PRAISE FOR
25 QUESTIONS GOD ASKED

"Mary Selzer paints pictures through her writing. The personal stories and biblical insights provide framework for powerful insights about coaching and the power of questions in the life of Christ, and the life of coaches and clients. Her artistry engages and challenges the reader in ways that births transforming insights. Thanks for sharing the journey with us, Mary!"
—Edward Hammett, Professional Certified Coach, Church & Clergy Coach, President of Transforming Solutions, LLC

"What makes a well-timed, well-framed question so powerful? (You *did* catch that I just asked a question, didn't you?) Questions capture our attention and promote discovery. They give an open invitation to response, exploration, and interaction. As a coach and mentor, I never cease to be amazed at how wrestling with a good question can move people forward toward their goals and dreams. But when GOD Himself is asking the question, that takes the significance and potential to learn, grow, and change to a whole new level. . . .

In this wonderful new book, *25 Questions God Asked: Discover the Answers that Will Change Your Life*, Mary has done us all a favor by exploring some of the powerful questions asked by an all-powerful God. She weaves compelling illustrations, helpful insights, and important cautionary tales that reveal the ramifications of those God-questions to our 21st century lives.

If, like me, you long to know God better and to know what He wants for and from you, put this book on your must-read list."
—Dr. Jodi Detrick, Speaker, Coach, Adjunct Professor, Author, *The Jesus-Hearted Woman: 10 Leadership Qualities for Enduring & Endearing Influence*

"Look no further! You could not purchase a more timely book, other than the Bible, than *25 Questions God Asked*. . . . We now live in a society that is no longer literate in the Bible in the way it was thirty years ago or more. One of the major barriers to people coming to Christ or being discipled is that they have a number of questions. What better way for ministers, coaches, and seekers to address this challenge than by reading a book of key questions and *answers* that the Lord provides."

—Dr. William Jeynes, Missionary/Evangelist;
Professor, California State University, Long Beach;
Senior Fellow, Witherspoon Institute, Princeton

"In her new book, *25 Questions God Asked: Discover the Answers that Will Change Your Life*, Mary Selzer illustrates how God, who truly knows our potential, uses questions to encourage reflections on our past and dreams for our future. While many are seeking for more answers, maybe those answers will emerge through divinely directed questions. God may have planted gifts and talents that are as yet undiscovered. Read this book and let the journey begin."

—Alton Garrison, Assistant General Superintendent,
The General Council of the Assemblies of God

"Mary Selzer; a deep believer, masterful coach, and engaging writer; has created a masterpiece by taking the Creator and Master's method of creating awareness and inspiring change and putting it in the book for us. This deep study of these 25 powerful questions provides insight into the original and most effective coaching methodology that exists. He created us and knows our " 'blueprint.' " Taking these questions into our own lives and professions enables us to remove the scales from our own eyes and opens the eyes and hearts of others. Asked in charity, they can do nothing but move us all " 'onward and upward.' " We all must study this book!"

—Colonel (Retired) John Moore, Professional Certified Coach,
CEO, and lover of our Lord

25 Questions
GOD
Asked

*Discover the Answers that
Will Change Your Life*

Mary Selzer

BARBOUR BOOKS
An Imprint of Barbour Publishing, Inc.

© 2016 by Mary K. Selzer

Print ISBN 978-1-63409-853-3

eBook Editions:
Adobe Digital Edition (.epub) 978-1-68322-060-2
Kindle and MobiPocket Edition (.prc) 978-1-68322-061-9

Published by Barbour Books, an imprint of Barbour Publishing, Inc., P.O. Box 719, Uhrichsville, Ohio 44683, www.barbourbooks.com

Our mission is to publish and distribute inspirational products offering exceptional value and biblical encouragement to the masses.

 Member of the
Evangelical Christian
Publishers Association

Printed in the United States of America.

To Lou, my husband
Rachel & Josh and Sarah & Jimmy, our kids
Zoey, Ava, Evelyn, James, and Juliette,
our grandkids and the joy of my life.

CONTENTS

FOREWORD

Every quest involves questions. The Christian quest is an adventurous journey toward life in God, toward knowing God and loving God, toward becoming the transformed kind of person who finds life with God natural and satisfying. Indeed, each of us who has found and is finding life in Christ is on a quest—a journey that does not cease with our first embrace of God's gift of grace, but continues as we move "onward and upward" as C. S. Lewis so poetically put it. Our quest is fueled by questions: questions we ask and questions asked of us.

Unfortunately, the church has too often ignored the wondrous power of questions. We have tended to prefer telling over asking, delivering over discovering, commanding over questioning. Certainly there is a need for strong delivery of truth, but there is also a need for compelling questions. Powerful questions are like sharp tools in the hands of a masterful craftsman. Questions can draw out wisdom, clarify truth, and even reveal ignorance.

As a professional coach and trainer of Christian coaches, I have seen firsthand how questions can help people see things differently, understand more deeply, act with intentionality, shift perspectives, and reach all kinds of goals. Coaches use many skills, but perhaps none is more crucial than asking powerful questions. While coaches embrace questions as a preferred way of engaging others, coaches are not the only ones who use questions to promote progress.

I teach coaching in a seminary setting, and often our coaching students are surprised when they realize how often Jesus asked questions and how many questions are asked throughout scripture. Once you have eyes to see the questions, you, too, might be surprised to realize how often God uses questions to fulfill His mission. Since scripture is God's perfectly revealed narrative—the truest story ever told—we should pay attention to the fact that scripture contains so many questions. The questions in the Bible not only move the scriptural story forward, but can also move our own stories forward—our personal story, the story of our church bodies, and the story of the world.

With the book you are holding, my friend and coaching colleague Mary Selzer has given the church a wonderful gift. For many years Mary has lovingly and painstakingly mined the Bible in search of the treasured questions found in God's Word. Her own quest in writing this book started with the question, "What are all the questions in the Bible, and what might they draw out of us?" I have found the questions of the Bible (as well as Mary's observations, reflections, and coaching questions) to be a powerful agent for change in my own life. I pray the same will be true for you.

Chad Hall, Master Certified Coach
Director of Coaching, Western Seminary

ACKNOWLEDGMENTS

So many people have influenced my life, encouraging me to stretch beyond my limits. Some of those individuals were key in the writing of this book:

- Coach Approach Ministries became my first introduction to coaching. Jane Creswell has inspired me in more ways than she knows. Chad Hall is fascinated with Bible questions even more than I am. Bill Copper taught me key coaching techniques when he served—and survived—as my very first coach.
- I don't know what I would have done without Dr. Janet Blakely, editor extraordinaire. She uses her red pen fearlessly, but she makes authors look good.
- My Christian Trinity Church family has encouraged, inspired, and motivated me. Thank you for allowing me to teach with questions. We may not have all the answers, but we have enjoyed countless explorations through the Bible.
- Annie Tipton, my editor at Barbour, has been a very present help in time of trouble. She always has a ready answer for my numerous questions.

INTRODUCTION

Several years ago, one of my coaching mentors, Jane Creswell, casually mentioned she was studying all of the questions Jesus asked. As a relatively new coach, I had discovered the impact of powerful questions, how they can create new awareness and stimulate the thought process. So, naturally, Jane's comment about the questions Jesus asked inspired me. *What about all the questions God asked?* I thought. *Or the questions Paul asked?* Suddenly, an idea exploded in my brain—*What about all the questions in the Bible?*

A few days later I grabbed my NIV Study Bible, opened to Genesis 1, and the search began. By the time I reached the final chapter in Revelation—more than a year later—I had painstakingly filled two spiral notebooks with a handwritten list of 3,241 questions, the names of nearly two hundred people who asked them, and the reason each question was asked. I spent several more months entering the data in the computer, sorting and categorizing the questions by topic and by who asked each question.

God asked nearly 14 percent of the questions recorded in scripture—450 powerful queries, many left unanswered because people were stunned into silence. He gave Jeremiah a wake-up call when he admonished, *"If you have raced with men on foot and they have worn you out, how can you compete with horses?"* (Jeremiah 12:5). Did God throw up His hands when He asked, *"What more could have been done for my vineyard than I have done for it?"* (Isaiah 5:4). Satan didn't know God was setting him up when He asked, *"Have you considered my servant Job?"* (Job 1:8).

Two of the questions posed by God really captured my attention because they were ones He *wished* someone had asked, but no one did: *"[The people] did not ask, 'Where is the LORD?'"* (Jeremiah 2:6). And, possibly worse—*"The priests did not ask, 'Where is the Lord?'"* (Jeremiah 2:8). Imagine how our lives could change if we ask the unasked question, *"Where is the LORD?"* each time we experience a tough situation or face a difficult decision.

My quest for Bible questions has opened up an entirely new way to study God's Word. These questions have become an inspiration around which I've developed teachings, sermons, and devotionals. The more I dig, the deeper I go. And the deeper I go, the more I discover about the character of God—a beautiful, unending journey in itself.

Take your time as you venture through *25 Questions God Asked*. I hope you emerge with keener insight about yourself, and even more about God, the Master of probing questions.

Mary Selzer

Chapter 1

SPIRITUAL CURIOSITY

*The priests did not ask,
"Where is the Lord?"*
Jeremiah 2:8

ASKED BY NOBODY

St. Patrick's Church in Cape Breton, Nova Scotia, has a sign in the front yard that reads ST. PATRICK'S CHURCH MUSEUM. The church has been out of commission since the 1960s. Tourists are regaled with stories about the good old days. Visitors *ooh* and *aah* over its unique, rustic decor and the glass cases exhibiting relics of the past. Except for a young tour guide and a native guitarist who belts out the island's national anthem, the building is cold and lifeless. From the outside, it still looks like a church. Even the name "St. Patrick's" speaks of a religious heritage. But standing inside the building, one can't help but ask, "Where is the Lord in this place?"

The Bible contains more than three thousand questions asked by nearly two hundred individuals. However, scripture records eight questions that nobody asked.[1] The fact that they are specifically recorded in the Bible as questions that were never asked indicates they are significant and merit our attention. One of those unasked queries is found in Jeremiah 2:8. Sadly, it was directed toward the priests—the spiritual leaders of the people.

The Lord was extremely concerned with how His people had forgotten the One who released

---

1. 2 Samuel 16:10; Job 35:10–11; Jeremiah 2:6, 8; 8:6; John 4:27; 21:12.

them from Egyptian bondage and brought them to their Promised Land. The spiritual leaders weren't any better than the people they led. God corrected them because they didn't even know God. In fact, some of the priests had defected from their holy calling to follow Baal (Jeremiah 2:8). The Lord called it appalling and horrific (Jeremiah 2:12). They had lost their spiritual curiosity and nobody asked, "Where is the Lord?"

Generations before, Moses, the leader of the Israelites, instructed them to "be careful, and watch yourselves closely so that you do not forget the things your eyes have seen or let them fade from your heart as long as you live. Teach them to your children and to their children after them" (Deuteronomy 4:9). Later he cautioned, "If you ever forget the Lord your God and follow other gods and worship and bow down to them, I testify against you today that you will surely be destroyed" (Deuteronomy 8:19). The people were to simply recall and retell. The leaders were to set the example.

Why would God give such a directive? I believe there are two reasons. First, when we see the Lord in every aspect of our lives, we will remain curious about where He will show up next. When we lose our spiritual curiosity, we will most likely lose our way. However, taking notice of God's whereabouts will boost our faith and give us something to bookmark and share.

The Old Testament records several times when something significant happened and the leaders commemorated the experience by building an altar. For example, when Jacob was reunited with Esau, he set up an altar and named it *Mighty is the God of Israel* (Genesis 33:20). Later he returned to Bethel and built another altar, calling it *God of Bethel* (Genesis 35:7), because God had revealed Himself to Jacob. After the Israelites experienced victory over the Amalekites as Moses' hands were held up by Aaron and Hur, Moses built an altar and called it *The LORD is my Banner* (Exodus 17:15). Gideon received such a flood of assurance from the Lord that he established an altar and named it *The LORD Is Peace* (Judges 6:24). The prophet Samuel set up a stone to mark the miraculous victory God gave the Israelites over the Philistines. He called the stone *Ebenezer—thus far the LORD has helped us* (1 Samuel 7:10–13). These were all significant experiences enjoyed for the moment and passed on for generations to come.

The second reason I believe God gave the instructions in Deuteronomy was for the leaders and the people to be accountable to each other. The leaders (priests, parents, teachers, etc.) should have accepted the responsibility to "be careful, and watch yourselves closely so that you do not forget the things your eyes have seen or let them fade from your heart as long as you live" (Deuteronomy 4:9). Then they would have had to be fully aware of who they followed and who followed them.

Many leaders have taught that every person should have a Paul, a Barnabas, and a Timothy in his or her life. "Paul" would serve as our mentor, someone we follow. "Barnabas" would be a co-laborer who sharpens our iron (Proverbs 27:17). "Timothy" would be a mentee who follows our example. When we are conscious of whom we follow, who follows us, and the responsibility we have to those individuals, we will remain aware of the Lord. It's perfect relational accountability designed by God.

The prophet Elisha knew the importance of acknowledging God and remaining spiritually curious, thanks to Elijah, his mentor. After Elijah was taken to heaven, Elisha picked up his dropped mantle. Standing at the bank of the Jordan, he struck the water with his mentor's cloak and asked the all-important question, "Where now is the LORD, the God of Elijah?" The river divided and he crossed over to the other side (see 2 Kings 2:13–14).

Elisha's question was both a statement and an act of faith. He had witnessed God's power at work in and through the life of Elijah, and he knew the same power was available for him to carry on the work started by his mentor. Notice that Elisha's first miracle was the same as the very last one performed by Elijah (see 2 Kings 2:8). The work of the Lord flowed seamlessly from one prophet to another because Elisha acknowledged what God had done and would continue to do.

The Lord doesn't want our lives to become museums of collected relics seen from a distance under protective glass. He wants our testimonies to be living stones that can be touched and felt and handled. When others see our Ebenezer stones, they will be encouraged to erect their own. Then the answer to "Where is the Lord?" will remain obvious—He is right here where He has always been.

QUESTIONS THAT GROW

- How do you bookmark significant events in your life? If you could give a name to your experiences, what would you call them? Do your children/grandchildren know your story?
- What stories are you keeping at a distance from others? How can you turn your relics into testimonies? Are you willing to open the glass case and let others have a closer look?
- If you are a leader and your followers ask, "Where is the Lord?" where would they

find Him in your life? How can you bring your Ebenezer stones back to life?

- Who is your Paul, your Barnabas, your Timothy?

Chapter 2

INVESTING IN INTEGRITY

*"Have you considered
my servant Job?"*
Job 1:8

Asked by God of Satan

The book of Job contains 288 questions, and more than a third of them were asked by God. His first two queries were directed to Satan at a time when the angels presented themselves before the Lord. "Where have you come from?" (Job 1:7); and "Have you considered my servant Job? There is no one on earth like him; he is blameless and upright, a man who fears God and shuns evil" (Job 1:8). Notice that God brought up Job's name first. Apparently He knew something about Job the devil did not.

God never gambles. He invests. Satan, however, enjoys an occasional wager, and this time was no different. "You have blessed the work of his hands . . . . But now stretch out your hand and strike everything he has, and he will surely curse you to your face" (Job 1:10–11). God gave Satan the green light to attack Job, but within limits, so Job himself would not be touched. Satan couldn't wait to go to work. Within twenty-four hours, Job lost it all—his children, his servants, and his numerous sheep, camels, oxen, and donkeys. The only thing he didn't lose was his trust in God. "The LORD gave and the LORD has taken away; may the name of the LORD be praised" (Job 1:21).

A second time Satan appeared before God. The

same dialogue ensued, only this time the Lord added, "[Job] is. . .a man who fears God and shuns evil. And he still maintains his integrity, though you incited me against him to ruin him without any reason" (Job 2:3). Satan challenged God again, and the Lord allowed him to touch Job physically, with the stipulation that his life be spared. Job's body became inflamed with painful sores from head to foot. And yet, scripture states, Job never sinned in what he said (see Job 2:10).

How did the Lord know Job would pass this horrific test? Apparently sometime in Job's life God had taken him for a few trial runs, and Job had succeeded. God doesn't test us to break us. He tests us to determine the strength of our character and the depth of our integrity, because He puts a high value on both. Job's wife, on the other hand, devalued Job's character when she challenged him, "Are you still maintaining your integrity? Curse God and die!" (Job 2:9). What wife doesn't want a husband of integrity? Apparently not Job's.

Simply put, integrity is an unbroken condition or "wholeness." When integrity is true, a person's private life will be in exact alignment with his public life. One man compared integrity to a person's shadow that is a perfect match to his body. Anything less is called duplicity or hypocrisy.

The story is told of a salesman who sat in the

purchasing agent's office, hoping to submit his company's bid. While he waited for the purchasing agent to return, he noticed a competitor's bid sitting on the desk. Unfortunately, the bid amount was covered by a Coke can. The salesman figured if he could see that number, he could underbid his competitor and win the sale. He gingerly picked up the Coke can and, to his dismay, hundreds of tiny pellets poured out from the bottomless can and scattered across the desk. Needless to say, he did not win the bid. The purchasing agent was looking for integrity, not an enticing offer.

God intends for us to be people of uncompromising character, and He tests us to achieve that goal. In Romans 5:3–4 Paul states, "We also glory in our sufferings, because we know that suffering produces perseverance; perseverance, character; and character, hope." It is through serious testing that we develop character. In the process, God continually keeps His hand on us to evaluate the depth of our morality and how much pressure we can withstand. He carefully monitors everything we experience.

The Department of Natural Resources has published principles for determining the "integrity" or depth of ice. For instance, when ice is only two inches thick, people are warned to stay off. Four-inch-thick ice can accommodate ice fishing and foot activities. When the depth reaches twelve to fifteen inches, a medium-sized truck can drive over it without danger. The greater the depth, the more pressure the ice can withstand.

The same idea applies to our character—the greater the depth, the more pressure we can withstand. How does God gauge our breaking point? Through trials. James said, "Consider it pure joy, my brothers and sisters, whenever you face trials of many kinds, because you know that the testing of your faith produces perseverance. Let perseverance finish its work so that you may be mature and complete, not lacking anything" (James 1:2–4). Mature people can endure tremendous amounts of tension, emerging from trials unscathed. Others require a warning sign—DANGER: THIN ICE—cautioning people to tread carefully due to fragile character.

God confidently allowed Satan to "drive his truck" over every part of Job's life because He was fully convinced of Job's ability to withstand a massive amount of pressure. The man never cracked, even under the most extenuating circumstances.

Satan had wagered and lost. As a result of Job's resolve, God restored to him twice as much as he had before. Although his net worth doubled, the true value was in the refinement process that caused him to emerge as gold (see Job 23:10). And the inheritance was passed on to his great-great-grandchildren—a legacy of integrity.

QUESTIONS THAT GROW

- Scripture indicates that Satan is still allowed to appear before the Lord (see Revelation 12:7–9). Does God have enough confidence in your level of integrity to mention your name to the devil? If not, what is missing in your life that God needs to see?
- How can you shift your focus to remember that when challenges come your way, the Lord is only testing you for a higher purpose? What do you need to do to consider your trials "pure joy"?
- When do you think our "trials of many kinds" will come to an end? At what point is a person considered "mature and complete, not lacking anything"? How does your response change your outlook on life?
- Think of trying times you have experienced in your life. What impurities did God remove so you emerged as "gold"? How can this realization change your attitude regarding trials yet to come?

Chapter 3

EMOTIONAL CHOICES

"If you do what is right,
will you not be accepted?"
GENESIS 4:7

ASKED BY GOD OF CAIN

In his book *The Winner Within*, basketball coach Pat Riley tells about the 1980–81 basketball season, when the Los Angeles Lakers were considered likely to win back-to-back championships. However, shortly after the season began, their star player, Magic Johnson, suffered a knee injury and was out of the game for three months. In spite of losing their best player, the rest of the team stepped up and played as hard as they could, winning 70 percent of the games.

As Magic's three-month recuperation period came to a close, the publicity became more focused on his return than on the winning team that had played successfully without him. During time-outs at the games, announcers would say, "Mark your calendars for February 27 when Magic Johnson returns to the lineup of your World Champion Los Angeles Lakers!" The other players would look up and curse. "We're winning *now*. What's so great about February 27?"

On February 27, all of the media attention focused on Magic Johnson's return. Ticket sales were through the roof, and press photographers vied for key spots on the floor to snap the first photo of Magic as he was announced. Someone said it was like a god returning to the crowd.

Meanwhile, the other team players were ignored. They seethed with jealousy, anger, and envy. The players became so resentful, they barely won the game that night, even though they played against the worst team in the league. Eventually, the morale of the entire team collapsed, the players turned on each other, and the coach was fired. The Lakers ended up with one of the most disastrous records ever. Coach Pat Riley said, "Because of greed, pettiness, and resentment, we executed one of the fastest falls from grace in NBA history. It was the Disease of Me."[2] Uncontrolled emotions cost the championship.

Our teenage daughters had the habit of taking their unbridled emotions out on their bedroom doors by slamming them as hard as they could. As parents, we countered by simply removing the doors for several days at a time. It wasn't long before our girls learned they needed to keep their frustrations in check or they would suffer the consequences.

When God created man, He included a healthy dose of emotions. No doubt Adam and Eve enjoyed peace, love, and joy in their picture-perfect garden. However, Adam may have shown a bit of loneliness before Eve was created, and the Lord took note. "It is not good for the man to be alone. I will make

2. Pat Riley, *The Winner Within—A Life Plan for Team Players* (New York: Berkley Books, 1994), 39–52.

a helper suitable for him" (Genesis 2:18). Imagine Adam's feelings of delight when he woke to discover the companion created exclusively for him.

Prior to the fall, the Bible gives no indication Adam and Eve felt any negative emotions. However, immediately after they sinned, they experienced a self-awareness that awakened feelings God did not intend, including shame and fear (see Genesis 2:25; 3:10). Their sin created a groundswell of negative emotions that affected generations to come with the "Disease of Me." Their firstborn son tasted jealousy, depression, and anger, causing him to lose control and make a regrettable choice.

Emotions are an important part of our makeup. Imagine living without the ability to laugh, convey joy, feel sadness, be annoyed, or express anger. However, we are to practice self-control, especially over negative emotions like fear, jealousy, and anger. For example, the Bible gives us permission to express anger, as long as we don't commit sin in the process. "In your anger do not sin; when you are on your beds, search your hearts and be silent" (Psalm 4:4 NIV 1984). Uncontrolled anger often leads to long-regretted decisions. For Cain, it started with sibling rivalry that turned deadly.

Bible scholars are not fully certain why God accepted Abel's offering and not Cain's (see Genesis 4:3–5). Some say the Lord was pleased with Abel's sacrifice because it involved the shedding of blood, pointing to Jesus' sacrifice. Others say Cain should not have brought the Lord a gift from the ground God had just cursed.

Discovering the reason why God rejected his offering is not as important as Cain's response to the rejection. Today, psychologists would probably diagnose Cain as lacking in "emotional intelligence." This term was coined by experts in the 1990s to describe a person's ability to identify and manage his own emotions. It's also the skill to recognize feelings in other people, cheering them up or calming them down as needed.[3] Abel apparently didn't pick up on his brother's dangerous mood, since he willingly went "out to the field" with him (see Genesis 4:8). And although Cain was warned by God, he refused to control his own internal frustrations, directing all of his jealousy and rage toward Abel. "Anger is cruel and fury overwhelming, but who can stand before jealousy?" (Proverbs 27:4). Cain lost control on both counts.

The Lord warned Cain about looming disaster if he didn't bring his anger and depression under control. "So Cain was very angry, and his face was downcast" (Genesis 4:5). God gave him an opportunity for a "do-over" so he could be in good

---

3. See "Emotional Intelligence," *Psychology Today*, www.psychologytoday.com/basics/emotional-intelligence.

graces with the Lord. "If you do what is right, will you not be accepted?" (Genesis 4:7). The Lord even cautioned Cain he would do something regretful if his emotions weren't kept in check. "If you do not do what is right, sin is crouching at your door" (Genesis 4:7). God knew that if Cain didn't control his emotions, they would control him. "[Sin] desires to have you, but you must rule over it" (Genesis 4:7). Rather than heed God's merciful warning, Cain allowed his strong feelings to turn to stubbornness. He relinquished control to a different master—sin that led him to murder his brother.

In a recent study about emotions, two researchers discovered that individuals who show anger are more likely to stubbornly support their initial decision, regardless of how wrong it may be. The researchers concluded that anger augments a sense of personal control, lowers perceptions of risk, and makes people less willing to admit mistakes.[4] We can see this evidence in Cain. When God confronted him with the whereabouts of Abel, Cain arrogantly responded, "I don't know. . . . Am I my brother's keeper?" (Genesis 4:9). Cain, the first man to experience birth, made his own brother the first human to experience death. His jealousy over Abel's

4. Ming-Hong Tsai and Maia J. Young, "Anger, Fear, and Escalation of Commitment," *Cognition and Emotion*, volume 24, no. 6, 2010, 962–73. www.tandfonline.com/doi/abs/10.1080/02699930903050631

favor with the Lord became the driving force that led him to a decision he regretted for the rest of his life (see Genesis 4:10–14).

In the end, everything pointed to the condition of the two brothers' hearts. In fact, John states in his epistle, "Why did [Cain] murder him? Because his own actions were evil and his brother's were righteous" (1 John 3:12). The writer to the Hebrews offers more clarification when he states that Abel's gift to God involved faith, but Cain's did not (see Hebrews 11:4). Abel apparently approached God with the right motives, but Cain's wicked heart caused him to make an irrational choice.

Expressing our emotions is normal. However, losing control leads to sin, and no one wins when sin is involved. Whether you lose a door, a game, or, worse, a brother, the price is too high to pay. Keep your emotions in check. Remember, sin is crouching at the door and it could be spreading the contagious "Disease of Me."

QUESTIONS THAT GROW

- What emotions do you have difficulty controlling? What scriptures can help you keep your emotions in check?
- What does God do to warn you that your emotions might be out of control? How do you respond to His warnings?

- Think back on emotional choices you've made. If God gave you a do-over, what would you do differently? How can your past decisions make a difference in how you make future decisions?

Chapter 4

GOD'S GESTATION PERIOD

*"Do I bring to the moment of
birth and not give delivery?"*
Isaiah 66:9

Asked by God of the Nation of Israel

At one minute after midnight on May 14, 1948, Israel made history. For centuries, the Israelites had been a people without a country, suffering under the rule of other empires like the Babylonians, the Persians, the Romans, and the Turks. In 1922 the League of Nations entrusted Britain with the Mandate for Palestine, recognizing "the historical connection of the Jewish people with Palestine."[5] Overnight that mandate expired and Israel was officially declared an independent Jewish state.

An article in the *New York Times* on May 15, 1948, stated, "The declaration of the new state by David Ben-Gurion, chairman of the National Council and the first premier of reborn Israel, was delivered. . .and new life was instilled into his people."[6] Israel had waited centuries to become a nation, but it was only a mere couple of days in God's eyes. "A thousand years in your sight are like a day that has just gone by" (Psalm 90:4).

God asked, "Can a country be born in a day or a nation be brought forth in a moment?" Now we know the answer. Yes! The waiting for Israel was finally over and a country was born.

In a natural pregnancy, crucial physical

5. See "British Palestine Mandate," Jewish Virtual Library, www.jewishvirtuallibrary.org/jsource/History/mandate3.html.
6. See learning.blogs.nytimes.com/2012/05/14/May-14-1948.

development occurs in the fetus during the forty-week gestation period. Today, thanks to technology, parents are privy to information about their unborn child long before its birth takes place. The child's gender can be learned, and multiple fetuses are detected so that parents can prepare for twins or triplets. In some cases, as long as the mother's health and the baby's development are normal, physicians allow the parents to select the day for the baby's arrival, using induction to deliver the child.

As useful as this technology may be, it has opened a controversial door for parental power in choosing abortion if defects are detected or, in extreme cases, for gender selection. Often these choices are made with little consideration of the consequences. Someone has said that knowledge is power. However, a misuse of knowledge will result in a misuse of power.

Our fast-paced world seems to increase the information highway at accelerating speeds. The more information we have available, the more control we have when making decisions. Informed decisions are good, but not when they interfere with obeying God in simple faith.

In pre-tech days, only God knew who was in the womb. David stated it beautifully in Psalm 139:15–16: "My frame was not hidden from you when I was made in the secret place, when I was woven together in the depths of the earth. Your eyes saw my unformed body; all the days ordained for me were written in your book before one of them came to be." Before we were born, God had already designed a divine plan for us. True obedience to the Lord means following that plan.

Is it possible we have become too rational when it comes to obeying God? We weigh the pros and cons, conduct surveys, and hire consultants. We analyze, design, and name before God's plan has had a chance to fully develop and be delivered. Unfortunately, the discovery phase in obeying God can lead us to a decision to abort the mission rather than await a full-term delivery. Too much analytical knowledge can destroy a decision that merely requires simple faith.

God doesn't always give us all the information we want, nor is He obligated to do so. Consider Abraham. At the age of seventy-five, God told him he would become the father of a great nation. However, God didn't tell him there would be a twenty-five-year gestation period. Abraham was one hundred years old when his son Isaac was born (Genesis 12:4; 21:5). Why did Abraham have to wait so long? Because the Lord wanted to test his faith so he would fully trust God instead of taking things into his own hands (see Hebrews 11:18–19).

What about Joseph? He had two dreams

indicating he would one day become a ruler. He spent his uncomfortable "pregnancy" first as a slave and then as a falsely accused prisoner. He carried that baby until he was thirty, when the fulfillment of his dream was birthed (Genesis 41:46). What happened while he waited? God prepared his heart to forgive his brothers and become a mature leader instead of a boy who merely dreamed.

David was anointed king of Israel as a teenager, and he spent his "pregnancy" running from the crazed King Saul. David's identity as the nation's leader wasn't realized until he reached the age of thirty (2 Samuel 5:4). Why so many years before he assumed the throne? God wanted him to be free of any animosity toward Saul and his family so the second king of Israel would indeed be a man after God's own heart (1 Samuel 13:14).

The human gestation period is nine months. But the spiritual gestation period is—well—variable. However, we can rest assured of this: when God conceives an idea in us, He will birth something great if we are willing to carry that baby to full development. Remember, "He who began a good work in you will carry it on to completion until the day of Christ Jesus" (Philippians 1:6).

God certainly knows how to deliver, doesn't He?

QUESTIONS THAT GROW

- Everyone agrees that premature babies are not healthy babies. How can you adjust to God's timetable and not give birth to one of His ideas before its time?
- Think of the last time you did something out of simple faith. How much information did you require? What kept you from overanalyzing?
- Have you ever "aborted" one of God's plans? What were the consequences? If you could go back, what would you do differently?
- What does God want to birth through you? How long have you waited? What changes are you experiencing while you wait?

Chapter 5

THE GREATEST TESTIMONY

"What fault did your fathers find in me, that they strayed so far from me? . . . Why do you go about so much, changing your ways?"
JEREMIAH 2:5, 36 NIV 1984

The man's story was captivating. As a child and young teenager, he had followed the Lord with a dedicated heart; however, when he reached early adulthood, unbelieving friends influenced him to choose a different path. After many wasted years of drugs, immorality, and crime, he called out to the Lord while in prison and God received him back. The contrast between his life of wickedness and God's restorative power was incredibly compelling.

After listening to the riveting testimony, I overheard some youth talking among themselves. Their words concerned me. "It's almost worth it to live a life of sin so you can have a great testimony," one reasoned as the others listened carefully to his logic. "You can relate to more people. And God would receive more glory through a person's sinful experience than through a man's boring Christian life." The others in his group nodded their heads in agreement.

Their conversation reminded me of my sophomore year in Bible college. Three classmates decided if they were going to have credible ministries, they needed incredible testimonies. All three of them had been raised in church. They were good ol' boys who had never done anything wrong—at least nothing that would merit them a platform and an audience. So all three decided to drop out of school and hit the streets in search of a plausible story to tell. Their logic was the same— *God will receive more glory if we intentionally sin and then return to the Lord.* One of them ended up strung out on drugs. Regrettably, none of them has yet returned to the Lord.

When God implements change, it is always for the good. It's not always so when man initiates change. Little wonder that God asked the Israelites, "Why do you go about so much, changing your ways?" (Jeremiah 2:36 NIV 1984).

From the beginning of their existence, the Israelites were told they had a choice to obey or disobey. God said one would be rewarded and the other would carry serious consequences. "See, I am setting before you today a blessing and a curse—the blessing if you obey the commands of the LORD your God that I am giving you today; the curse if you disobey the commands of the LORD your God and turn from the way that I command you today by following other gods, which you have not known" (Deuteronomy 11:26–28). Unfortunately, the people chose disobedience, and they missed the ultimate blessings of God, causing Him to ask, "What fault did your fathers find in me, that they strayed so far from me?" (Jeremiah 2:5 NIV 1984).

What brings God the most glory: a

demonstration of His keeping power or His redemptive power? The answer is both. It depends on where a person begins his relationship with the Lord. Some folks are raised in a godly culture, experiencing a healthy spiritual upbringing. Others are less fortunate and don't learn about the Lord until later in life. Scripture makes it clear, however, that we are all born into sin. "Surely I was sinful at birth, sinful from the time my mother conceived me" (Psalm 51:5). If we are all born into sin, then we are all susceptible to temptation. Some people battle sins of the flesh that are manifested externally. Others experience internal struggles, such as pride or a critical spirit. External sins are easier to identify, while internal offenses can be concealed. Whether internal or external, they're all sins requiring repentance.

I was raised in a godly home by parents who taught my siblings and me to fear and love the Lord. I was a pretty good kid who attended church regularly and participated in all of the programs for children and youth. I grew up thinking sin was identified only by an external manifestation—offenses of the flesh like smoking, drinking, drugs, immorality, rock and roll, inappropriate dress, cussing, etc. I was oblivious to the fact that pride (possibly the worst sin of all) had crept into my heart. I let my lifestyle become the standard by which everyone else was measured.

After graduating from Bible college, I joined the staff of Teen Challenge, a Christian residential program for people with life-controlling problems. Most of the students had been involved in drugs, alcohol, or other external deviant behavior. I remember arriving on the Teen Challenge property thinking to myself, *Teen Challenge is so blessed to have me here. I've never smoked, drunk, or gotten high on drugs. I'm pure and virtuous. What a blessing I'm going to be to this ministry.* Then an unbelievable thought entered my mind: *Compared to the unfortunate students in this program, I'm perfect!* Little did I know that God had a program designed especially for "perfect" people. His program saved my life.

Our Teen Challenge center had a choir that ministered in various churches. I often accompanied them on the piano. At one church service, I was playing the piano following the sermon, and the Lord clearly spoke to my heart: "Kneel down and pray." I responded, "I can't. I'm playing the piano right now." He became more insistent with me and I reluctantly stopped playing and knelt by the piano bench. Arrogantly I said, "All right, God. I'm kneeling. Now what do You want from me?" "I want you to ask Me what you look like to Me," He directed. "That's easy," I retorted. "I'm perfect and sinless, and I'm more than happy to see what You see."

God began to play a video of my life, showing me the pride, judgmentalism, and stubbornness that had built up in my heart over the years. I wept uncontrollably as I realized my sin was greater than that of the ex–drug addicts with whom I worked. At least they had humbled themselves before the Lord as they recognized their need for God. I had seen no need of the Lord in my life because I thought I had reached spiritual perfection. My smugness had crowded Him out. How many times had He tried to ask me, "What fault do you find in Me, that you strayed so far from Me?"

Whose testimony brings the most glory to God—someone delivered from a shattered lifestyle of addictions, or a person set free from the bondage of spiritual pride? They both do!

The most powerful spoken testimonies are distinct in two ways. First, they show a clear contrast between the old lifestyle and a miraculous change to the new. "Therefore, if anyone is in Christ, the new creation has come: The old has gone, the new is here!" (2 Corinthians 5:17). Second, the most powerful testimonies carry impact whether spoken before an audience of one thousand or one. The psalmist said, "On my bed I remember you; I think of you through the watches of the night. Because you are my help, I sing in the shadow of your wings" (Psalm 63:6–7). Nothing compares with those intimate moments with God when we acknowledge Him for changing in us what no one else knew needed to be changed. It's the greatest testimony.

And when God hears us express our gratitude to Him, He applauds.

QUESTIONS THAT GROW

- What is the testimony of contrast in your life? From _____ to _____?
- What are you trying to change in your life that only God can change? How can you relinquish control?
- When was the last time you shared your testimony privately with God? If you sit quietly, He will reveal the significant changes He has made in your life. Enjoy the moment and then give your applause to God.

Chapter 6

LEARNING TO ENDURE

"If you have raced with men on foot and they have worn you out, how can you compete with horses?"
Jeremiah 12:5

ASKED BY GOD OF JEREMIAH

In 1973 Secretariat, one of the greatest thorough-breds of all time, set a record by running one mile in a little over one and a half minutes! That's twice as fast as Hicham El Guerrouj, a Moroccan knight who holds the record for running a mile in 3:43:13.[7] Obviously, a horse can easily outrun a human in speed sprints. But when it comes to long distances, humans have been known to actually out-endure horses.

Endurance is the ability to exert oneself or to remain active over a period of time; it is also the ability to withstand fatigue, stress, or pain. Paul said, "We...glory in our sufferings, because we know that suffering produces perseverance; perseverance, character; and character, hope. And hope does not put us to shame" (Romans 5:3–5). Any suffering we experience is necessary for us to learn to persevere. The fruit of perseverance is character, which gives us hope.

Joni Eareckson Tada's life is a perfect example of perseverance. At the age of seventeen, Joni became a quadriplegic as the result of a diving accident. Over the years, she has learned to endure incredible pain and difficulty. Her persistence has enabled her to become an internationally known

7. "Mile Run," *Wikipedia*, last modified June 1, 2016, https://wikipedia.org/wiki/Mile_run.

speaker, singer, author, and artist (by holding a brush in her mouth). She founded Joni & Friends, a ministry offering Christ-centered programs and services to meet the practical and spiritual needs of disabled people and their families.

For nearly five decades, Joni has positively affected millions of individuals as she has shown endurance in the midst of hardship. She says, "I believe that God's purpose in my accident was to turn a stubborn kid into a woman who would reflect patience, endurance, and a lively, optimistic hope of the heavenly glories above."[8] Joni may not be able to walk, but she certainly competes with horses—and wins!

It doesn't take much to quit. But it takes a lot to persevere—especially when you feel alone or abandoned. God wanted Jeremiah to press on, even when he thought he had no allies.

Jeremiah was God's mouthpiece to warn the nation of Israel about the consequences of their unfaithfulness. His prophecies included a warning that Israel would be taken captive by the Babylonians and held for seventy years. Jeremiah may not have been the bearer of good news, but he was the teller of truth. However, instead of repenting and turning back to God, the people

---

8. Joni Eareckson Tada, "A Victory through Suffering," http://powertochange.com/discover/faith/jeareckson.

rejected the warning and plotted to kill him (see Jeremiah 11:19, 21).

At one point, Jeremiah became so discouraged he complained to God, "I would speak with you about your justice: Why does the way of the wicked prosper? Why do all the faithless live at ease? . . . You are always on their lips but far from their hearts. . . . Drag them off like sheep to be butchered! Set them apart for the day of slaughter! . . . Because those who live in [the land] are wicked, the animals and birds have perished. Moreover, the people are saying, 'He will not see what happens to us'" (Jeremiah 12:1–4).

God challenged, "If you have raced with men on foot and they have worn you out, how can you compete with horses?" In other words, if Jeremiah couldn't handle a few threats for speaking the truth (short sprint), what would he do when his endurance was tested—like being locked in a vaulted cell in a dungeon (Jeremiah 37:16), or being lowered into a mud-filled cistern (Jeremiah 38:6)? Even worse, Jeremiah would soon witness the fulfillment of the prophecies with his own eyes. What could be worse than watching your beloved people be taken captive by the dreaded enemy? Jeremiah was devastated and he wept bitterly over the demise of the great nation of Israel (Lamentations 3:48–49). The short sprints were over. Now it was time for the marathon.

Ironically, God instructed him to tell the people not to resist going into captivity, but instead: "Build houses and settle down; plant gardens and eat what they produce. Marry and have sons and daughters. . . . Increase in number there; do not decrease. Also, seek the peace and prosperity of the city to which I have carried you into exile. Pray to the LORD for it, because if it prospers, you too will prosper" (Jeremiah 29:5–7). The Lord intended for the people to be content and prosper in adverse circumstances!

Just before the Israelites were taken captive, God told Jeremiah to encourage the people with this promise: "'When seventy years are completed for Babylon, I will come to you and fulfill my good promise to bring you back to this place. For I know the plans I have for you. . .plans to prosper you and not to harm you, plans to give you hope and a future'" (Jeremiah 29:10–11)—a seventy-year endurance stretch with hope at the finish line. The Lord was true to His word, and the Israelites returned to their abandoned land to rebuild and replenish (see Isaiah 44:26).

In the book of Revelation, the apostle John prophesied about horses that symbolize war, violence, famine, death, and martyrdom in the end times (Revelation 6:2–8). Although some debate whether the book of Revelation is figurative or literal, one thing we know for certain: the closer we get to the coming of the Lord, the more challenging it will be to stay the course. Jesus cautioned His disciples, "Because of the increase of wickedness, the love of most will grow cold, but the one who stands firm to the end will be saved" (Matthew 24:12–13). Our reassurance is what Paul calls our "blessed hope"—the coming of the Lord (Titus 2:13).

Let's modify an old saying: "When the going gets tough, the tough run with horses." It will be a challenging marathon, but our "blessed hope" awaits us at the finish line.

QUESTIONS THAT GROW

- God's question to Jeremiah uses two different words—*race* and *compete*. What is the difference? How does preparing for a *run* differ from preparing for a *competition*?
- The words of people were keeping Jeremiah from running as he should. How do the words of people slow you down? What can you do to keep yourself from being wrongly influenced?
- How is training for speed different from training for endurance? What similarities can be applied to a person's spiritual growth?

Are you a spiritual speed runner or a spiritual endurance runner?

- Read 1 Corinthians 9:24–27. What truths can be gleaned from this passage as ways to prepare for "competing with horses"?
- Where do you find it the most challenging to endure? What do you need in order to make it to the finish line?

Chapter 7

LOCKED IN LOVE

*This is what the L*ORD *says: "Where is your mother's certificate of divorce with which I sent her away? Or to which of my creditors did I sell you?"*
ISAIAH 50:1

Asked by God of Israel

In 2006 Italian author Federico Moccia published a novel about a couple who attach a lock to Rome's Ponte Milvio Bridge and throw the key into the river, symbolizing their undying love for each other. The night before his book was published, Moccia actually placed a lock on the Ponte Milvio Bridge, just in case readers would check to see if the tradition was real. Within days, three hundred locks were added to the bridge.[9] Since then, the idea has spread throughout the world as thousands of couples inscribe their names and a date on padlocks, attaching the symbols to a bridge while tossing the keys into the water.

However, what was once a moving act of love has evolved into a major problem for cities everywhere because the weight of the locks is causing serious damage to the bridges. In Paris, a portion of a bridge actually collapsed under the weight of the love locks. To the consternation of devoted couples, many municipalities have found it necessary to remove the love lock structures for safety reasons. One city is replacing the metal grilles on the bridges with lock-proof Plexiglas panels to prevent lovers from attaching their love symbols on the edifice.

9. Elena Berton, " 'Love Locks' Scourge of Bridges Worldwide," *USA Today News*, June 5, 2015.

When asked what would happen if a couple broke up, divorced, or found someone else, a "love-lock guardian" shrugged and said, "I suppose one of them could come at night with lock cutters, bust it apart, and throw it in the water." So much for undying love.

God intended marriage to be a lifelong relationship. However, because people's hearts were hard and stubborn, Moses permitted married couples to divorce (see Matthew 19:8). The husband was required to present his wife a "bill of divorcement" that reversed the original marriage contract. As much as the Lord is concerned about marital divorce, He is equally—if not more so—concerned about spiritual divorce because it carries eternal consequences.

The relationship between God and the Israelite people was unique, stemming all the way back to His covenant with Abraham (see Genesis 15:18; 17:4–7). The Lord often referred to it as a type of marriage relationship (see Isaiah 54:5; Jeremiah 3:14; Ezekiel 16:32). While God remained faithful to them, the Israelites had a wandering eye that found other gods more attractive and appealing than the one true God. Unfaithfulness was an incessant problem for the Jewish people. In fact, throughout the prophetic books, the Lord addresses their unfaithfulness and often refers to the Israelites as adulterous people (see Jeremiah 3:8; Ezekiel 23:37; Hosea 4:14).

God desired a simple love relationship with the Israelites. However, they became locked into man-made traditions that led to legalistic lifestyles devoid of much-needed internal change. They preferred offering sacrifices over demonstrating broken and contrite hearts (Psalm 51:17); they traded justice for impressive offerings and celebrations (Amos 5:22–24); they ignored mercy and humility in hopes of pleasing God with their massive gifts (Micah 6:6–8); instead of loosing chains of injustice and liberating people from their oppression, they turned their spiritual disciplines (like fasting) into times of quarreling and strife (Isaiah 58:4–7). All God wanted was faithfulness.

The Lord never deviated from His covenant relationship with the people. Man, on the other hand, became restless, dissatisfied, and distant. Soon the religious leaders stepped up and created their own dos and don'ts in an effort to please themselves, almost taking the place of God. Dr. Joseph M. Stowell, former president of Moody Bible Institute, stated:

> *In contrast to the two commands of Christ, the Pharisees had developed a system of 613 laws, 365 negative commands, and 248 positive laws. By the time Christ came, it had produced a heartless, cold, and arrogant brand*

*of righteousness. As such, it contained at least
ten tragic flaws. (1) New laws continually
needed to be invented for new situations.
(2) Accountability to God was replaced by
accountability to men. (3) It reduced a person's
ability to personally discern. (4) It created a
judgmental spirit. (5) The Pharisees confused
personal preferences with divine law. (6) It
produced inconsistencies. (7) It created a false
standard of righteousness. (8) It became a
burden to the Jews. (9) It was strictly external.
(10) It was rejected by Christ.*[10]

Small wonder that Jesus cautioned His disciples,
"[The teachers of the law and the Pharisees] tie up
heavy, cumbersome loads and put them on other
people's shoulders, but they themselves are not
willing to lift a finger to move them" (Matthew
23:4). The teachings of the rabbis—also known
as "yokes"—were laden with laws and rules that
God never intended. The religious leaders added
more and more weight to their teachings, and the
people dutifully carried out the expectations of their
instructors in an effort to please and oblige.

Jesus brought much-needed relief when He
said, "Take my yoke [teaching] upon you and learn
from me, for I am gentle and humble in heart, and

---

10. Joseph M. Stowell, *Fan the Flame* (Chicago: Moody, 1986), 52.

you will find rest for your souls. For my yoke is easy and my burden is light" (Matthew 11:29–30). No more heavy tradition. Not even a symbolic lock on a bridge that can collapse from the weight of man-made customs. Just a simple love relationship.

The only symbol we need is the permanent structure God erected—a cross that signifies His undying love. Jesus is the key that frees us to receive God's unconditional love. And we never need to fear being served with a certificate of divorce, because nothing can separate us from the love of God in Christ Jesus our Lord (Romans 8:38–39).

QUESTIONS THAT GROW

- In Jeremiah 3:11, God called Israel "faithless" and He called Judah "unfaithful." What is the difference between being faithless and unfaithful? How does either one affect our relationship with God?
- What is something the Lord allowed you to do because you were insistent? If you could have a do-over, what would you do differently?
- What rules or expectations do people bring on themselves that God never intended? How can people be released from these traditions?

- How difficult—or easy—is it for you to accept the yoke that Jesus offers? What heavy load will you give up in exchange for His light burden?

Chapter 8

THE NAME CHANGER

"What is your name?"
GENESIS 32:27

ASKED BY GOD OF JACOB

Maximus Julius Pauson, who lives in New York, was not given a name at birth and went without one for nineteen years. His birth certificate simply read "Baby boy. Name to come." The name never came. People informally called him Max after his mother, Maxine. His teen years were rocky as he dabbled in drugs and spent time in foster homes. His interests were eclectic, including fascination with authors Dr. Seuss and C. S. Lewis, as well as a variety of artists. The time came for Max to apply for his first job, but he needed a mandatory background check. In order to do that, he had to establish an identity. So Max was allowed to choose his own name. He selected a memorable, dignified one—Maximus Julius Pauson. Today he is a celebrated artist and is extremely pleased with the name he gave himself.[11]

When it comes to naming their babies, parents often select names according to family tradition or current trend. One new mother's mind went blank when she was asked to name her newborn daughter. So she asked her doctor, "What's your wife's name?" "Wilma," he replied. "Then that will be my baby's name."

It's not unusual for some people to pick up a nickname based on personality or physical traits. A

11. Erik Eckholm, "What's in a Name?" *New York Times*, May 10, 2010, A12.

red-haired boy may end up being called Rusty, or a son named after his father might be called Junior. Sometimes a nickname carries more significance than the name given at birth. For instance, Tiger Woods's legal name is Eldrick. His father had called an army buddy responsible for saving his life "Tiger" and ended up passing the nickname on to his son.

In Bible days, names were often given to children based on the circumstances at the time of birth. Hannah named her son Samuel ("heard of God") because she had prayed fervently for a son (see 1 Samuel 1:20). Leah named her firstborn Reuben ("the Lord has seen my misery") because she was not loved by her husband (see Genesis 29:31–32). Pity Eli's grandson who was born the fateful night the ark of the covenant was captured by the Philistines. Just before she died in childbirth, the mother named her child Ichabod, lamenting, "The glory of the Lord has departed from Israel" (see 1 Samuel 4:12–21). I believe I would have preferred a nickname.

Jacob and Esau were named according to what took place at their birth. Esau, the firstborn, came out red and hairy and was immediately given a name that means "red." However, when Jacob emerged, his hand was clutching Esau's foot. The midwife saw this as a possible sign that Jacob might try to deceive or overpower his older brother. Thus the name Jacob, which means "deceiver" (see Genesis 25:21–26).

Throughout the book of Genesis we read stories about how Jacob lived up to his name. He tricked his brother out of his birthright (Genesis 25:29–34). He deceived his own father by pretending he was Esau in order to receive the family blessing intended for the oldest child (Genesis 27:1–40). He outwitted his father-in-law and added to his own wealth by taking more sheep than were intended for him to have (Genesis 30:25–43).

Jacob certainly became what he was called—*a deceiver*. So it was no small thing when God wrestled him to a place of reality and asked him to say his name. Jacob blurted out, "My name is deceiver." That was enough for God to hear. "Your name will no longer be Jacob, but Israel" (Genesis 32:28–32). During the wrestling match, God wrenched Jacob's hip, leaving him with a permanent limp. God didn't just change Jacob's name. He changed his walk.

Names and their meanings are significant to God. Consider the names Hosea was instructed to give his children. His two sons were named to represent Israel's pathetic spiritual state at that time: *Lo-Ruhamah* (Not Loved) and *Lo-Ammi* (Not My People). Later the names were changed to *Loved*

One and *You Are My People*, displaying God's love
and redemption at work (Hosea 1:6, 9; 2:1). The
entire nation of Israel experienced a new identity
when the Lord assured them, "No longer will they
call you Deserted or name your land Desolate. But
you will be called Hephzibah, and your land Beulah;
for the LORD will take delight in you, and your land
will be married" (Isaiah 62:4). God is the Name
Changer!

Sometimes the Lord just wants a person to
live up to his given name, if it's worth living up
to. Take Gideon, for example. His name actually
means "mighty warrior." His clan was the weakest
in his tribe, and he was the least in his family. So
who in the world named him *Mighty Warrior* if he
was the least? When the angel of the Lord found
him, Gideon was hiding in a winepress to avoid the
Midianites. The angel called him by his name—
Mighty Warrior—and gave him an assignment that
matched his name. The results? The Mighty Warrior
led the Israelites to a mighty victory (see Judges 6–7).

Unfortunately, some people carry labels because
of poor choices they've made. One woman whose
husband had been a heroin addict for years found
it nearly impossible to get help for him. Time
after time medical professionals told her that his
situation was hopeless. "Once a junkie, always
a junkie," they said. Finally, a Christian friend

encouraged him to enter a Christian rehabilitation program. Imagine the freedom the husband and wife both experienced when they were exposed to God's redemptive hand and the power of His Word. The "junkie" label was gone forever. "Therefore, if anyone is in Christ, the new creation has come: The old has gone, the new is here!" (2 Corinthians 5:17).

Even you and I will receive a new name—a secret nickname given by God Himself. The Lord reveals in Revelation 2:17 that when we arrive in heaven, He will give those who overcome a white stone with a *new name* written on it. That name will be known only to the One who gives it and the one who receives it. What an amazing, intimate welcome into eternal life!

What is *your* name?

QUESTIONS THAT GROW

- If your family or friends gave you a name based on your personality, what do you think they would call you? What do you *want* them to know you as? What has to change for you to merit that name?
- Have you ever wrestled with God? Who won? How did your walk change after that wrestling match?

- What labels are you still carrying from the past? How do you think God sees you? What do you need to do in order to accept *His* truth and lose the labels?
- What criteria do you think the Lord uses when He gives us a nickname?

Chapter 9

SPIRITUAL AFFLUENZA

*"How long will these people treat
me with contempt? How long
will they refuse to believe in me,
in spite of all the signs I have
performed among them?"*
Numbers 14:11

In 2013 sixteen-year-old Ethan Couch slammed his truck into a group of people who were helping a woman with a stalled vehicle. Four individuals were killed and nine others were injured. Ethan was traveling thirty miles over the speed limit and his blood alcohol level was three times the legal amount.[12] A psychologist who testified at the trial described Ethan as suffering from "affluenza": *extreme materialism and consumerism associated with the pursuit of wealth and success and resulting in a life of chronic dissatisfaction, debt, overwork, stress, and impaired relationships.*[13]

The teen's attorneys grabbed onto the affluenza defense. They claimed Ethan wasn't responsible for his actions because his rich parents spoiled him by giving him "freedoms no young person should have."[14] The line of defense worked. Despite public outcry, Ethan avoided a possible twenty-year prison sentence and instead was placed on ten years' probation. Ethan Couch and his affluenza defense

12. Gary Strauss, "No Jail for 'Affluenza' Teen in Fatal Crash Draws Outrage," *USA Today*, February 6, 2014, http://www.usatoday.com/story/news/nation/2014/02/05/no-jail-for-teen/5242173.
13. merriam-webster.com/dictionary/affluenza.
14. Helen Pow, "Drunk Driving Teen Who Killed Four Is Spared Jail 'Because He's Rich,'" *Daily Mail*, December 11, 2013, http://www.dailymail.co.uk/news/article-2521743/Ethan-Couch.

will remain in legal infamy for years to come. However, this question remains unanswered: Who is to blame—Ethan or his parents?

Although the term *affluenza* was coined in the twentieth century, the symptoms can be traced back to Bible days. Consider these similarities between the children of Israel and Ethan Couch: they were never satisfied, they cast blame on others, and they struggled against the boundaries established for their own protection. The difference between Ethan and the Israelites is that, unlike Ethan's wealthy parents, God didn't spoil His children. He blessed them.

The Lord had miraculously delivered the children of Israel from Egyptian slavery and moved them toward the Promised Land—a land filled with rich potential. He called it the land flowing with milk and honey (Exodus 3:8). From the time the Israelites left Egypt and arrived at the border of the Promised Land—despite their numerous complaints—the Lord generously provided for their needs and performed numerous miracles:

- He led them with a cloud by day and a pillar of fire by night (Exodus 13:22; Numbers 9:15–23).
- He miraculously parted the Red Sea and they crossed over on dry ground (Exodus 14:21–22).

- The bitter waters of Marah were made sweet (Exodus 15:24–25).
- The Lord provided manna in the middle of the desert (Exodus 16:2–4).
- He brought water from a rock (Exodus 17:2–6).
- They defeated the Amalekites (Exodus 17:8–16).
- God gave them the Ten Commandments and established protective rules, guidelines, and boundaries by which they were to live, setting them apart from other nations (Exodus 20:1–21).
- He miraculously drove in quail from the sea (Numbers 11:4–6, 31–32).

When the Israelites found themselves on the border of Canaan, God instructed Moses to send one representative from each of the twelve tribes to scout out the land. For forty days, the twelve men spied and made mental notes. They returned to camp with an impressive sample of fruit and conflicting stories. Ten spies were alarmists who informed the people that the land "devours those living in it. All the people we saw there are of great size. We saw the Nephilim there.... We seemed like grasshoppers in our own eyes, and we looked the same to them" (Numbers 13:32–33).

Joshua and Caleb countered the negative report, contending they could indeed conquer the land, regardless of the size of the people. "Their protection is gone, but the LORD is with us. Do not be afraid of them" (Numbers 14:9). It might be a difficult challenge, but God would lead them to victory.

Throughout their desert journey, the Lord was faithful to show His power to His people. However, instead of acknowledging the Lord's impressive track record, the Israelites resorted to what they did best—complaining. God responded by asking Moses, "How long will these people treat me with contempt? How long will they refuse to believe in me, in spite of all the signs I have performed among them?" (Numbers 14:11).

The Hebrew meaning for the word *contempt* is "to scorn or reject." It carries the idea of a relationship where one person rebels after being shown favorable attention.[15] We would refer to such a person as being ungrateful, unappreciative, or thankless. What more could the Lord have done for these people? Apparently safe travel, victorious warfare, and miraculous food weren't enough. Instead of moving ahead into the Promised Land,

---

15. Spiros Zodhiates, *The Hebrew-Greek Key Study Bible* (Chattanooga: AMG Publishers, 1991), 1,633.

the complaining children rejected God's best and cried out to return to Egypt. Who was to blame for their spiritual affluenza? Certainly not God.

Psychologists claim that some wealthy children actually despise the way they were raised. One reason is their parents didn't say no enough. Another is that wealthy parents are often absent parents, and the kids feel abandoned. Although our God is incredibly wealthy, He doesn't raise His children in this fashion. The Lord has no problem saying no when He knows something is not the best for us. Nor does He abandon us, but instead promises He will never leave us (Deuteronomy 31:8). What more does the Lord have to do for us?

I once heard a minister pray, "Father, if You never answer another prayer for us, the gift of Your Son dying on the cross is sufficient." When I heard him pray these words, I fervently nodded in agreement. Naturally, when things are going well and we are pain-free, problem-free, and poverty-free, it's easy to say, "Lord, You've done enough for me." But try keeping that attitude when prayers go unanswered or our world seems to fall apart. Discomfort and disappointment can cause us to forget how blessed we really are. If we suffer from spiritual affluenza, who's to blame? Certainly not God.

People face serious consequences for ungrateful attitudes. The Israelites had to wait forty years before they could approach the Promised Land again. They were condemned to wander in the desert until the last of that complaining generation died (Numbers 14:29–35). If only they had remained faithful and acknowledged the Lord, the history of Israel would have been significantly different.

God is a perfect parent who wants His children to learn contentment, take responsibility for their actions, and live within His protective boundaries. If we can trust Him when He keeps us from freedoms we should not have and do not need, we will never treat Him with contempt. Instead we will rest secure in a loving parental relationship with our heavenly Father.

Questions That Grow

- If God never answers another prayer for you, would you be content with what He has already done for you? If not, what will make you content?
- What can you do to continually remain aware of God's work in your life?
- How do you respond when God tells you no? How can you begin to acknowledge it as a blessing from Him?
- What spiritual implications can you find

in the definition of affluenza—"extreme materialism and consumerism associated with the pursuit of wealth and success and resulting in a life of chronic dissatisfaction, debt, overwork, stress, and impaired relationships"? What would be a good cure?

- How would you describe your relationship with the heavenly Father? How can your relationship with Him be strengthened?

Chapter 10

RECONCILING DEBT

"What else can they sleep in?"
Exodus 22:27

ASKED BY GOD OF THE ISRAELITE PEOPLE

Two homeless men were deep in conversation.
They stuffed their flimsy plastic bags with what
few belongings they owned while discussing their
daily dilemma. "Where should we spend the day?"
one asked, while he nervously eyed the inclement
weather. "Let's use our bus passes and ride the bus
downtown," the other offered. "That's fine. But where
will we sleep tonight?" "Did you forget?" his friend
reminded him. "We're coming back to this shelter.
It's a warm place to sleep, and we'll get a hot meal."

My heart went out to these men, and I felt a
bit of shame as I listened to their conversation. My
daily dilemma is how I will accomplish everything
on my to-do list, while theirs revolves around
simple survival.

For years, our church has been one of several in
the community that serves as a homeless "warming
center" during the winter months. We've hosted
as many as one hundred guests on a given night.
Each person has a story, and the stories carry the
same theme—at one time they all had a family, a
home, and possessions, but at some point, they were
stripped of their dignity, pride, and self-worth.

It is true that a few homeless have burned
their bridges and, for whatever reason, prefer
living on the streets. Others, however, experienced

the misfortune of job loss, home eviction, or acrimonious divorce, and they have been left destitute. It's one thing for a person to bring misfortune upon himself; it's quite another for someone else to be the cause of one's impoverishment. God does not look too kindly on people who take advantage of those who are less fortunate.

In Exodus 22, God instructed the Israelites about their social responsibility to one another. "Do not mistreat or oppress a foreigner, for you were foreigners in Egypt. Do not take advantage of the widow or the fatherless," He cautioned (Exodus 22:21–22). The Lord also touched on the subject of making loans, instructing the people not to charge interest—or at least not to charge exorbitant rates (Exodus 22:25). Apparently some folks were so desperate for money that they would offer the shirts—their cloaks—off their backs as pledges to repay their loans.

In Bible days, people owned cloaks that served a dual purpose. During the day, they wore the capes as outer garments. Then in the evening, the same cloaks served as blankets to keep them warm. If a person borrowed money, he would offer his cloak as collateral. However, the Lord instructed the lender to return it by evening; otherwise, "What else can he sleep in?" Imagine a person tossing and turning on his bed without a cloak to keep him warm, his shivering body serving as a reminder of his debt. The Lord seemed more concerned about the borrower enjoying a good night's sleep than He was about repayment of the loan.

The scripture passage in Exodus 22 addresses two groups of people—borrowers and lenders. Notice the Lord doesn't infer that the borrower never has to repay the loan. When He instructs the lender to return the cloak as pledge, He is implying that the borrower's word should be good enough. He should pay what he owes so he can sleep with a clear conscience.

Sleep is a gift from God (Psalm 127:2). The Lord knows our bodies and minds need a refreshing reprieve from the daily grind. Thank God He invented sleep! We should protect it for ourselves and for others. We can rob ourselves of the gift of sleep in two ways:

1. We fail to pay our debts. Not all debts are financial. We might owe an apology, an explanation, forgiveness, or a long-overdue favor. Our debts should be paid in a timely manner. When we don't pay what we owe, relational reconciliation becomes the emotional cloak we willingly give up as collateral. Then what will we sleep in?

2. We hold someone else's emotional cloak
    as collateral. The Lord instructed, "If you
    take your neighbor's cloak as a pledge,
    return it by sunset" (Exodus 22:26). In
    other words, don't hold on to something
    that serves as a continual reminder of what
    you think you are owed. Some people find
    it easier to hold on to an offense than to
    release it. An unreleased offense becomes
    an emotional debt that, held over time, can
    increase in size. This is not unlike a money
    lender who adds exorbitant interest to a
    loan. Increasing an offense becomes a type
    of emotional and mental usury. The irony is
    that both the borrower and the lender can
    lose sleep over the same offense.

God knows our human tendency to hold on to
things longer than we should. So He instructed the
Israelites that every seven years they were to cancel
debts owed by their fellow Israelites. It was called
"the LORD's time for canceling debts" or, as another
version puts it, "the time of the Lord's release"
(Deuteronomy 15:2).

If someone is losing sleep because of a "debt"
we are holding over their head, we need to consider
a time of canceling that debt. If canceling a debt
of money was important to God, how much more

should we be willing to cancel debts of forgiveness so we can be reconciled?

One homeless man discovered the power of reconciliation. He had lost everything because of his alcohol addiction. His marriage was ruined and his teenage son rejected him. The loss of his well-paying job became the final blow that sent him to the homeless warming center. He entered as a broken, despondent man, devoid of his cloak of dignity. Each night, he was served a hot meal, and he attended a Bible study taught by one of the volunteers. Then he found his spot on the floor where he wrapped himself in the two blankets allotted each guest.

One night he responded to the tug of God's grace on his heart, asking the Lord to remove his desire for alcohol and to restore his relationship with his son. On the following Sunday, his son met him at church where they were tearfully reunited. His son canceled the debt of offense and returned the emotional cloak he had held as collateral. The father repaid the debt by keeping his promise to give up alcohol and become a responsible parent. Today, he is employed and living in an apartment with his son. What do they sleep in? The comfort of reconciliation.

Whether you are a borrower who owes someone something or a lender who is holding

someone else's emotional cloak, do what you can to
reconcile with your neighbor. Otherwise, what will
you sleep in?

QUESTIONS THAT GROW

- Are you holding someone else's "cloak"?
  How can you return it?
- Who has taken your "cloak"? If they don't
  return it, how will you guard your heart?
- What keeps you awake at night? How can
  you release your concern and accept, as
  God's beloved, His gift of sleep?
- What debt (besides financial) do you owe?
  What will it cost you to balance the books?
  If you don't pay what you owe, what will you
  sleep in?

Chapter 11

RELEASING GRUDGES

*"Are you repaying me for
something I have done?"*
Joel 3:4

ASKED BY GOD OF THE PEOPLE OF TYRE, SIDON, AND THE REGIONS OF PHILISTIA

If you are like me, your initial response to this question might be, "Who would even think about paying the Lord back for something we think He has done wrong?" God's question to the people of Tyre and Sidon—"Are you repaying me for something I have done?"—isn't absurd; but the fact that He had to ask it *is* absurd. First, God has never done anything to merit being repaid for a wrongdoing. Second, what prideful spirit would provoke a nation—or a person—to even think He deserves payment for what might be considered wrong behavior?

The inhabitants of Tyre and Sidon held an offense against God because He had corrected them. The truth is, they deserved to be corrected. These people had gambled (cast lots) for the Israelites, exploited children in unimaginable ways, and robbed God in order to supply their own godless temples (Joel 3:3, 5–6). They even had the nerve to rejoice when Jerusalem was overtaken (Ezekiel 26:2). The Lord, in His mercy, gave fair warning they would be judged. However, instead of repenting, they projected their anger toward God in an attempt to "pay Him back." The Lord cautioned them, "If you are paying me back, I will swiftly and speedily return on your own heads what you have done" (Joel 3:4).

It's difficult to respond in a proper manner when we receive correction, isn't it? We can become defensive—and even resistant—when confronted about a wrongdoing. Those who are wise will not disregard corrective words. Solomon said, "He who ignores discipline despises himself, but whoever heeds correction gains understanding" (Proverbs 15:32 NIV 1984). The more we welcome correction, the more our hearts will be protected (see Proverbs 2:11). If we reject correction, we will also be forfeiting understanding, creating an open door through which offenses can easily enter.

If offenses are not dealt with immediately, they can fester and eventually develop into grudges. Grudges demand retribution. We "repay" offenders in different ways. We can snub, we can withhold something, or we can treat people vindictively. Sometimes we broaden the scope of the offense by maligning the offender's character to others.

The unavoidable reality is that life is going to be filled with offenses. How we respond to those offenses determines how long (or short) a grudge will live. We can feed it by rehearsing and nursing the offense. Or we can release the grudge and let it die. Fortunately, if we don't recognize an offense immediately, God in His mercy will reveal it to us. He doesn't want us to carry grudges, and He certainly is more eager to show His kindness than His wrath (see Psalm 86:15). Regrettably, some people who don't understand God's character may attempt to pay Him back for what they consider to be unfair treatment. A person might withhold obedience or acts of worship when disappointed over unanswered prayers or what seems like an unreasonably tough trial. But paybacks—whether to God or man—will end up costing much more than we ever expected to pay.

One of my college professors claimed to be an agnostic. When he learned I was a Christian, he made it a point to publicly confront what he considered "flaws" in my beliefs. In one class he challenged, "If your God is so loving, why did He let my mother die of multiple sclerosis—especially after I prayed diligently for her to be healed?" It was obvious he carried an offense against the Lord and he wanted to take it out on someone.

Later, in a private conversation, he admitted that, years before, he had attended seminary to prepare for the priesthood. However, after the Lord failed to heal his mother, he chose "wine, women, and song" (his words) and renounced God's existence in a feeble attempt to pay Him back. Holding the offense may have given him gratification that he was punishing God. The harsh reality was that he paid a hefty price by missing out on God's best for his life.

In the Gospel of Mark, we read the story of Herodias, who "nursed a grudge against John [the Baptist] and wanted to kill him" because he confronted Herod about unlawfully marrying Herodias, his own sister-in-law (see Mark 6:14–19). Herod didn't take offense when corrected. However, Herodias picked up the offense and turned it into a grudge. She coerced Herod to have John imprisoned and eventually beheaded. In fact, Mark specifically states, "Herodias nursed a grudge against John and wanted to kill him. But she was not able to" (Mark 6:19). If Herodias "nursed" that grudge, she must have devoted a lot of time and effort to keep it alive.

If anyone deserved to hold a grudge, it was Joseph (see Genesis 37–50). This poor guy was sold into slavery by his jealous brothers. He was falsely accused and served a prison sentence he didn't deserve. Through the mercy of God, he went from serving in prison to serving Pharaoh as second in command over Egypt, navigating that country through a severe famine. When his brothers made their way to Egypt to get food, they were shocked to learn Joseph was still alive. Even more stunning was Joseph's willingness to forgive them because he saw God's hand in everything that had happened to him (Genesis 45:5–7).

His brothers breathed easier—that is, until their father, Jacob, died. They thought Joseph was being kind to them only because Jacob was alive. They panicked. "What if Joseph holds a grudge against us and pays us back for all the wrongs we did to him?" (Genesis 50:15). When Joseph learned of their concern, he wept. He had every right to see that his brothers paid for their actions. But Joseph chose to cancel their debt through forgiveness. God repaid Joseph by softening his heart and enabling him to see his circumstances from a different vantage point. Joseph repaid his brothers with reassurance: "You intended to harm me, but God intended it for good" (Genesis 50:20). What a perfect example of forgiveness!

When we deal with offenses, maybe all we need is a softer heart and a broader vision, like Joseph. In the end, it is God who pays back—fair and square. He will extend judgment to those who deserve it (Isaiah 59:18; Jeremiah 16:18; Joel 3:4), and He will repay His children for what they may have unfairly experienced (2 Samuel 16:12; Joel 2:25; 2 Thessalonians 1:6). We can find comfort that no matter what others do to harm us, God will turn it around for good. Not only does the Lord pay our debts, but His books always balance.

QUESTIONS THAT GROW

- What is the difference between "forgiving" and "not holding a grudge"? What steps have you taken in the past to release grudges? What grudges might you be holding now that need to be released?
- What are ways people repay God? How does it affect their relationship with Him? How would you counsel someone who felt God deserves to be repaid?
- How have you seen people nurse grudges? What happens to a grudge when it is nursed? How can an offense be allowed to die?
- How do you think the story of Joseph might have ended if he had taken revenge? What kept him from repaying his brothers?

Chapter 12

ASKING THE RIGHT QUESTION

*"[The people] did not ask, 'Where is the L*ORD*, who brought us up out of Egypt and led us through the barren wilderness, through a land of deserts and ravines, a land of drought and utter darkness, a land where no one travels and no one lives?'"*
JEREMIAH 2:6

Coach trainers teach the skill of asking powerful questions centered around a client's desired agenda and outcome. Sometimes the client and the coach get stuck and aren't sure what to do next. One way to help the client get "unstuck" is to say, "What question would you like me to ask that will help you right now?" Often the person's eyes light up and he throws out the perfect statement, leading him to gain new awareness. It's all about asking the right question.

The query posed in Jeremiah 2:6 is one of eight "unasked" questions recorded in scripture. God hoped someone would ask because He considered the question extremely important. If the Israelites had inquired of God, "What question would You like us to ask?" He probably would have responded, "Ask Me, 'Where are You, Lord?'" Then their focus would have been redirected toward Him. Sadly, the Israelites had lost not only the presence of the Lord; they had lost curiosity about knowing where He was. They didn't care enough to even ask.

Generations earlier, Moses had cautioned the Israelites, "Acknowledge and take to heart this day that the LORD is God in heaven above and on the earth below. There is no other. Keep his decrees and commands, which I am giving you today, so that it may go well with you and your children after you and that you may live long in the land the LORD your God gives you for all time" (Deuteronomy 4:39–40). The Israelites failed to *acknowledge*, *take to heart*, and *keep* those instructions. Now they had lost both God's presence and the Promised Land. Spiritual apathy had destroyed any desire or curiosity they might have had about the presence of the Lord.

The Lord charged the people of Israel with two specific sins (see Jeremiah 2:13):

1. *They forsook Him as their spring of living water.* Over the years, God had shown Himself to be their provision for every need. They didn't have to work for what He gave. They only had to obey and drink from a refreshing spring that never ran dry. God was no doubt scratching His omniscient head when He asked, "What fault did your ancestors find in me, that they strayed so far from me? They followed worthless idols and became worthless themselves" (Jeremiah 2:5). The Lord had given the Israelites everything they needed for physical and spiritual sustenance. Instead, they chose to drink the bitter water from their own man-made gods that resulted in illusory hope and discontentment.

2. *They dug their own broken cisterns that could not hold water.* Water cannot flow in a cistern. A cistern only collects as much (or as little) as the rainfall gives. Why did the people go to the trouble of digging a cistern if the spring of living water was

available? First, they forgot the Lord who was their sovereign leader and had faithfully led them for generations. Second, they lost their desire for the Lord and created their own recipe to quench their thirst. Sadly, what they made with their own hands couldn't hold enough to satisfy anyone. Apparently, they forgot Solomon's caution to "trust in the LORD with all your heart and lean not on your own understanding; in all your ways submit to him, and he will make your paths straight. Do not be wise in your own eyes; fear the LORD and shun evil" (Proverbs 3:5–7).

God wanted the people to remember that although they traveled through "barren wilderness, through a land of deserts and ravines, a land of drought and utter darkness, a land where no one travels and no one lives," there was hope on the other side—a fertile land of rich produce (Jeremiah 2:6–7). How soon they forgot God's faithfulness. How quickly they deserted the Lord. No one asked, and no one cared.

Life will have times when it feels like we're in the middle of nowhere—dark, scary, desolate moments when clouds of discouragement hover above in an effort to keep us from seeing God. Those are the times we need to acknowledge His presence and cry out, "Where is the Lord?" He will always respond and lead us past the land of barrenness into His orchard of bountiful fruit. It's when we follow our own ways that we remain stuck in a hopeless, unproductive wilderness.

One young woman who grew up in the church had a passion for the Lord. She was determined to follow the Lord wherever He led. The pastor affirmed that the Lord's hand was indeed on her life. "But," he cautioned, "the devil will want to destroy you. Keep your eyes on the Lord. He will protect you and you will do great things for His kingdom."

Instead of taking her leader's advice, she reasoned within herself that the devil would remain distant if she compromised her commitment to the Lord. She rejected the spring of living water by digging her own cistern of logic in an attempt to appease Satan. The devil took full advantage of her decision, and for the next seventeen years, he made sure she drank from her self-made container—bitter water of dissatisfaction and disappointment.

Fortunately, she had a praying mother who knew how to ask, "Where is the God who has His hand on my daughter's life?" In her mid-thirties, the young woman turned her back on the man-made cisterns and returned to the spring of living water. Over the years, she has worked through the regrets, and God has repaired, replenished, and restored her hope for the future (see Jeremiah 29:11).

When we remove the blockage of "my way" and release the flow of "His way," He will show up in every part of our lives. We just need to be curious and ask the right question: *Where is the Lord?*

QUESTIONS THAT GROW

- What needs to be removed so God can flow through your life?
- Some people say we should never question God because it indicates we don't trust Him. What do you think?
- Have you ever dug a cistern of your own will? What ended up filling that cistern? What happened to you as you drank its contents? What brought you back to the Living Water?
- If you asked God what question(s) He would like you to ask Him, how would He respond? What questions would you like to ask God but have been afraid to?

Chapter 13

THROWING IT ALL DOWN

"What is that in your hand?"
Exodus 4:2

ASKED BY GOD OF MOSES

Moses was born during a time of slavery. The Israelites had been living—and multiplying—in the land of Egypt after escaping a severe famine (see Genesis 41–47). A new pharaoh, who didn't know the full history of how the Israelites came to Egypt, stepped into power. Threatened by the steadily increasing number of Israelites, Pharaoh put Egyptian slave masters in charge to work them ruthlessly. Even under brutal circumstances, the Israelites continued to multiply. In an attempt to control the growing Hebrew population, Pharaoh ordered all male babies be thrown into the Nile River.

This was the world into which Moses was born. His mother risked her life and saved his when she hid him in a waterproof basket on the bank of the Nile. Pharaoh's daughter found him and raised him in the palace.

When Moses was around forty years old, he killed an Egyptian after he witnessed him mercilessly beating a Hebrew. Pharaoh heard what Moses had done and tried to have him killed. Moses fled for his life and ended up in Midian, where he married the daughter of a priest and became a shepherd. That's when Moses found his staff. Little did he realize the significance of that simple piece of wood.

In its natural state, the shepherd's staff was a vital piece of equipment, used to corral, count, and protect the sheep. No shepherd could work without one. The staff served as protection and security for both the sheep and the shepherd—in its natural state. But in its *supernatural* state, that simple piece of wood could demonstrate the power of God. And the Lord intended to do exactly that—through Moses.

For forty years Moses was a sheep-leading desert nomad. His vision was limited to his flock and survival. No doubt the memories of life in the Egyptian palace had all but faded and the sandy expanse had become a comfort zone. The farther he moved the sheep in the desert, the more distance he put between himself and his land of birth (see Exodus 3:1). Life had a routine and Moses was content to keep it that way. But God had other plans for the eighty-year-old shepherd.

"I am sending you to Pharaoh to bring my people the Israelites out of Egypt," God announced one day (Exodus 3:10). Moses stuttered and stammered and gave every excuse why he couldn't/ shouldn't return to Egypt. Then the Lord directed his attention to what he held in his hand. This one piece of equipment was about to take on new significance.

"Throw it on the ground," God told him. When he did, the staff turned into a snake (Exodus 4:3).

The Lord told him to grab it by the tail and see what would happen. The snake turned back into a staff. Moses would never look at that staff—or his life—the same again. God turned his predictable routine upside down by supernaturally using what he already possessed.

A new revelation demands renewed responsibility. God can help us see our workplace as a chance to share His peace rather than a space where we simply earn a living. He wants to show us that a relationship we thought had died can be brought back to life if we will take the first step toward reconciliation. He might want us to view our difficult circumstance as a stepping-stone toward growth rather than a stumbling block toward failure. It all depends on how we look at it. Do we see a staff or a snake?

Imagine Pharaoh's astonishment as Moses wielded the rod under God's direction and ten plagues poured out on the land of Egypt (Exodus 7–10). The Israelites watched in awe as Moses used it to strike the Red Sea, and later a rock in the desert, indicating God's power over the water (Exodus 17:5–7). The Amalekites must have recognized the *presence* represented in the staff when they lost to the Israelites as Moses held it high during their battle (Exodus 17:8–16). The Israelites might not have had a flag of victory, but

Moses waved that pole as a signal of triumph for the Israelites.

Did the staff itself possess power? Of course not. It was an instrument God used to show His might. God can use anyone anywhere to accomplish anything.

Maybe what you have in your hand isn't a pole. It might be a pink slip from work. You could be clutching memories from your childhood. Perhaps a bad report from the doctor makes your hands shake. Whatever it is, "throw it on the ground" and see what God does with it. He might send you on a mission.

My cousin had just retired from her job and was preparing to enjoy a cruise with some friends. But God had other plans. During a routine physical exam, she received the devastating news that she had a quick-spreading cancer, and the prognosis was not good.

God: *"What do you have in your hand?"*
Cousin: *"The X-ray from the radiologist."*
God: *"Throw it on the ground."*

She did. When I called to offer some encouragement, her response amazed me: "I'm doing great. I told God that whatever His plan was for my life, no matter how brief, I'll do anything He wants. My life isn't mine anyway. It's His. Besides, my oncologist isn't a believer. If my having cancer is what will put me in his office to witness to him, then I'm willing to walk that path."

Before beginning chemo treatments, she took three brief trips to visit people she had met and witnessed to on previous vacations. My cousin spent time with each one to secure their eternal future before she faced hers. She faithfully witnessed to the oncologist, his team, and countless others the Lord put in her path before calling her home. She threw her sickness on the ground, and the Lord used the opportunity to grant eternal life to many who otherwise might not have heard.

What is that in *your* hand? Throw it down and watch God work.

QUESTIONS THAT GROW

- What are you clutching tightly that God wants you to throw on the ground? What are you afraid will happen when you do?
- Sometimes the routine of life can become our comfort zone. How does the Lord stretch you? What excuses do you make when He tries?
- How has the way you were raised affected your life now? Instead of using your past as a stumbling block, how can you turn it into a stepping-stone?

- God called Moses to accomplish what seemed an impossible mission. When the Lord asks you to do something beyond your ability, how does He empower you? How willing are you to let the Lord take something natural and perform the supernatural?

Chapter 14

ANTICIPATING DEATH

"Where, O death, is your victory?
Where, O death, is your sting?"
1 Corinthians 15:55

ASKED BY GOD OF DEATH

A children's Sunday school teacher asked his class, "Will a person go to heaven because he gets all As on his report cards?"

"No!" the class responded.

"Will he go to heaven because he helps his mom around the house?"

"No!"

"Will he go to heaven because he never fights with his sister?"

"No!" they shouted.

"Then what does a person have to do to go to heaven?"

A young girl responded, "Ya gotta die first."

Death is a journey we will all have to take someday. Many people—including some Christians—find it a morbid subject, and some consider it "bad luck" to talk about death. We are on this side of heaven and see death from an earthly perspective with a limited view. Death seems dark and depressing.

But those believers who have already taken the journey through death into eternal life see it from an enlightened perspective. Ask anyone who has died before us if they would trade the peace and beauty of heaven for the pain and turmoil of the world. I doubt there would be any takers.

One person told me he wasn't afraid of death, but he was deathly afraid of dying. Death is instantaneous—we are alive one moment and dead the next. Dying, on the other hand, can be a long and sometimes unpleasant process. What if we consider death the destination and dying the journey we take to get to the destination? That might be something we can live with.

In our family, one of the best parts of taking a trip, especially to a new place, is the preparation and anticipation before the vacation even happens. We envision what the location looks like, browse through brochures, and plan side excursions. Everything from planning to packing builds the anticipation. When the day of departure finally arrives, everyone is excited and ready to roll. We may not have all the information about our destination, but we have a pretty good idea, thanks to the travel brochures.

We've discovered that some advertisements build more anticipation than the actual destination deserves, and we've had a few disappointing trips. On the other hand, some brochures just don't do the destination justice. More than once, we've been astounded with the stunning beauty and awe of various locations we've visited. How can a simple brochure do justice to the Mayon Volcano in the Philippines or the Amboseli National Park in Kenya?

The Bible's description of heaven isn't as detailed as we would like. No doubt it was intentional on God's part so we would live with the anticipation of our future home. He gave us a couple of chapters in the book of Revelation with a description that leaves us with more questions than answers. *Will we recognize each other in heaven? What will we do all day? Will we remember what we did on earth? Are we going to float on clouds and play harps?*

I believe the Lord enjoys it when we imagine what heaven will be like, because it means we are excited about spending eternity with Him. Imagine our exhilaration when we discover how the breathtaking reality of heaven far surpasses what the human mind ever could have dreamed or imagined. Maybe we need to fear less and dream more.

If death is the momentary transition from earth to heaven, then dying is the journey we take to get there. For some, it's a long trip, like an extensive illness. The thought of dying without dignity can be daunting. We can find comfort when we remember that God is sovereign and everything He does is done with dignity. His own children are not exempt from suffering, sickness, or pain. Remember what the Lord told Paul after he pleaded three times for his thorn in the flesh to be removed: "My grace is sufficient for you, for my power is made perfect in weakness" (2 Corinthians 12:9). God's grace and power will reduce our pain and discomfort, making those difficulties bearable. *Where, O death, is your sting?* He minimizes the pain of death to less than an insect sting.

Once I was stung four times on the arm by an angry wasp. The stings hurt, but the pain was bearable. It brought tears to my eyes for a minute. An ice pack alleviated the soreness and, in time, I forgot that I was ever stung. If the only way to get to heaven is that "ya gotta die first," then the Lord will allow the Christian to have a bright, joyful, and sting-free experience. We might have tears for a minute, but His grace alleviates the pain. Consider the dying words of these heroes of the faith:

- D. L. Moody, American evangelist: "If this is death, it is sweet! God is calling me and I must go."
- Adoniram Judson, missionary to Burma: "I go with the gladness of a boy bounding away from school. I feel so strong in Christ."
- John A. Lyth, Methodist lay minister: "Can this be death? Why, it is better than living! Tell them I die happy in Jesus."
- Charles Spurgeon, British preacher: "This is my coronation day. I can see the chariots, I'm ready to board."

We may not have a say in the mode of transportation—but we do get to pick our final destination.

The Bible mentions the word *death* more than 365 times—one for at least every day of the year! Maybe it's a reminder that life is short. For the Christian, God not only sends escorting angels when we die (see Luke 16:22), but Jesus accompanies us. He said, "Never will I leave you; never will I forsake you" (Hebrews 13:5). Jesus didn't just conquer death—He made it so impotent that death stings less than a wasp! Our bodies may suffer on the journey, but He provided the way for us to take the trip with peace, comfort, and confidence. Maybe "ya gotta die first." But remember, "Precious in the sight of the LORD is the death of his faithful servants" (Psalm 116:15).

Are you packed yet?

QUESTIONS THAT GROW

- What did the psalmist mean when he said the death of saints is precious in the sight of the Lord? How can death become precious to you?
- What scares you the most about dying or death? What steps can you take to turn that fear into anticipation of your arrival in heaven?

- How does the death of someone close to you affect your attitude toward death and dying? If you are still grieving, what hope do you have to comfort your heart?
- What can you do to help others find peace about dying and death? How can you prepare yourself to have a ready answer for everyone?

Chapter 15

WHERE IS GOD?

"Am I only a God nearby. . .
and not a God far away?"
JEREMIAH 23:23

When our oldest daughter was a baby, we took her for regular checkups with the pediatrician. While we waited in the examining room, I would entertain my daughter with toys, making her giggle and laugh. Eventually, we would hear the doctor's footsteps outside the door. Sometimes he would pause in the hallway for several seconds before entering the room. I couldn't see him, but I knew he was near. "It sounds like you're having fun in here," he said one time as he opened the door. A few times he stood across the room and talked to my daughter from a distance. At first I found it a little unusual until I realized he was more engaged than I realized.

While the doctor was standing across the room, he was observing my daughter's vision and hearing. Could she turn her head in the direction of his voice? Did her eyes focus correctly? Was I, the mother, connecting well with my child? He may have stood at a distance, but he was very present.

In his book *When God Shows Up*, Dr. R. T. Kendall defines spirituality as "the ability to close the gap between the time of the Lord's appearance and our being aware that it is the Lord."[16] God does show up in every situation. We just may not be spiritually attuned enough to recognize Him. If

16. R. T. Kendall, *When God Shows Up* (Ventura, CA: Gospel Light, 1998), 44.

we can close the gap between feelings and trust, we will be able to sense God's presence sooner. As we spiritually mature, we realize that as long as God can see us, He is close enough (see Jeremiah 23:24). And since we are always within His sight, He is always present.

The nation of Israel was facing serious consequences for its spiritual unfaithfulness. Jeremiah had warned the people multiple times that God would send them into Babylonian captivity if they didn't repent. The prophet certainly didn't make the people feel very good about their future. At the same time, dishonest prophets countered Jeremiah's words by promising peace and safety, giving the people false hope. These same false prophets were living double lives, committing adultery without shame and encouraging evildoers to continue in their wicked ways. The Lord called them godless and wicked, declaring they would face punishment for how they were misleading the people (Jeremiah 23:11–13).

Naturally, the people found it much more appealing to believe the comforting lies of the prophets than to heed the warning of the one who really spoke for God. Why should they let one man shake their world while all the other prophets spoke messages of peace and prosperity? As long as the leaders spoke confidently of tranquility, the people could rest well. God would never let their nation be taken captive—at least that's what the seers said.

Then God ruined their human logic: "'Am I only a God nearby,' declares the LORD, 'and not a God far away? Who can hide in secret places so that I cannot see them? . . . Do not I fill heaven and earth?'" (Jeremiah 23:23–24). His words combined a revelation with a promise. Yes, He was a God in Jerusalem. But He also filled the entire universe by His omnipresence. Even if the Israelites were taken to a faraway land, the Lord would be just as near as if they were all meeting together in the temple at Jerusalem.

What devotion God had to His people! The Israelites were rebellious, wicked, and resistant to the truth. Yet the Lord gave assurance He would remain with them no matter where they might end up. Jeremiah encouraged the Israelites that even if they were held in a faraway land against their will, they could still seek God—and they would find Him (see Jeremiah 29:13). But first they had to seek. Fortunately, some of the Israelites took God at His word and sought Him in a foreign land.

Not long after Jeremiah's warning about Babylonian captivity, his prophecy was indeed fulfilled. Among those captured in the first deportation were four young men named Daniel, Shadrach, Meshach, and Abednego. These men knew how to seek God (see Daniel 2:17–23), and they found Him in the land of captivity.

Shortly after their arrival in Babylon, Daniel discovered that the Lord was still in full control when He used Nebuchadnezzar to elevate Daniel to a position of great power and influence (Daniel 2:48). When Shadrach, Meshach, and Abednego refused to worship Nebuchadnezzar's statue in Babylon, they found the Lord in the midst of the raging furnace and emerged without even the smell of smoke (Daniel 3:25–28). Several years later, Daniel was thrown to the lions for refusing to obey the king's command to cease his daily time of seeking God. Daniel's persistence helped him find the Lord among the hungry beasts, and he emerged unscathed (Daniel 6:23).

One wonders what impact the words Moses spoke centuries earlier had on these four young men: "Be strong and courageous. Do not be afraid or terrified because of them, for the LORD your God goes with you; he will never leave you nor forsake you" (Deuteronomy 31:6). He was indeed a God nearby in a faraway land.

We may not be in physical confinement to an enemy, but sometimes our own thoughts and doubts can enslave us to the lie that God is distant. If we seek Him, we will find Him, just as He promised. As we remain persistent, we will discover that He's closer than we think.

Questions That Grow

- If you had been an Israelite under the influence of the prophets, would you have pushed back against their false prophecies? What are ways a person can discern whether a word is truly from the Lord?

- Some people use the term "praying through"—the process of staying in the presence of the Lord until they sense a breakthrough. What difference would "praying through" make compared to those times when someone would act without prayer? Why do some people find "praying through" laborious?

- How can we close the gap between the time God shows up and when we are aware of the Lord's presence? How big is your spiritual gap? What will you do to close it?

Chapter 16

THE PARADOX OF HUMILITY

*"Have you noticed how
Ahab has humbled himself?"*
1 KINGS 21:29

Jose[17] was a member of one of the most notorious gangs in the country. He spent his teen and early adult years involved in drug dealing, gang warfare, and serious crimes—including murder. Jose had spent some years in jail for the lesser crimes, but he was never caught for killing.

A local pastor was able to establish a relationship with Jose and, after a period of time, led him to the Lord and encouraged him to enter a Christian drug rehabilitation program. Jose did well in the program and, at one point, felt God calling him to become a full-time minister.

However, Jose had a skeleton in his closet— murder. A few months before graduating from the rehabilitation program, he told one of the staff members, "I think I need to turn myself in and face the consequences for my crime." The staff member asked him if he realized he would face possible prison time. "If I am going to be a minister for the Lord, I need to have a clear conscience. I'm willing to take the gamble."

At his graduation from the program, staff gathered around Jose and prayed for God's will to be done. He returned to his hometown and turned himself in to the police. They immediately

17. Not his real name.

arrested him and, following court proceedings, he was sentenced to several years in prison. While incarcerated, Jose started a Bible study and ended up leading many inmates and guards to the Lord. By the time he completed his prison term, he emerged a different man—and the prison was never the same because of his godly influence. Upon his release, the Lord opened doors of ministry for Jose that would not have opened had he not taken responsibility for his actions.

What enabled Jose to make such a crucial decision and emerge a stronger man? Godly sorrow. He was sincerely sorry for his misdeeds, and he was willing to face the consequences. Unfortunately, not everyone is as responsive as Jose.

King Ahab was also a notorious character. He and his wife, Jezebel, comprised an infamous gang of two. Ahab might have been the king, but Jezebel called the shots. Ahab was content to comply with her wishes. During their reign, hundreds of people were murdered at Jezebel's command while Ahab watched the bloodshed from the sidelines (see 1 Kings 18:4; 21:10, 25). After the death of innocent Naboth, God had seen enough. He instructed Elijah to inform the wicked king that his day of reckoning was near. As soon as Ahab heard the warning, he "tore his clothes, put on sackcloth and fasted. He lay in sackcloth and went around meekly" (1 Kings 21:27). Too bad he didn't repent. Things might have turned out better for him and his family.

While Jose sincerely repented of his ways, Ahab was only sorry he got caught.

Godly humility is a paradox. James said, "Humble yourselves before the Lord, and he will lift you up" (James 4:10). The lower we bring ourselves before the Lord, the higher He will lift us. However, He will raise us to the level of His standards, not ours. If we are truly humble, we will be satisfied with where God brings us. Man's standard of elevation will become trivial.

Every few years, my husband and I enjoy a cruise. We have been on a total of six, and the cruise line has raised us to the "Gold" level. We were impressed with our status until we learned from other passengers that Gold was actually at the bottom of the heap. We met Diamond and Platinum people—those who had cruised enough times to merit special amenities. But the most coveted is the "Pinnacle" status. Pinnacle people sport shiny pins heralding their rank. They are sent to the front of the lines; they've all shaken the captain's hand, and they're invited to eat with him at the Captain's Table.

On one particular cruise, my husband and I were standing in line to enter the dining room for breakfast. A Diamond person asked me my level. "Gold," I responded. Looking down her nose at me, she said, "Didn't you know that Gold people are supposed to eat upstairs with the Pinnacle people? Although," she added, "I have no idea why the ship would allow the Golds to eat with the Pinnacles." "Why not?" I asked. "It's all the same food, just eaten one level up." "Harrumph," she snorted as she scurried to the front of the line.

Yes indeed. Man's elevation process certainly can be trivial. But man's promotions are often founded on ego. God's basis for lifting people up is humility, not pride.

Scripture is very clear about the need for humility and how it can be achieved. We can either humble ourselves voluntarily (see 2 Chronicles 7:14; Zephaniah 2:3; Ephesians 4:2; James 4:10; 1 Peter 3:8; 5:5–6), or we can be humbled by the hand of God (Deuteronomy 8:2–3; 1 Kings 11:39; Psalm 18:27; Isaiah 13:11; Daniel 4:37). I prefer the first option. When we choose to humble ourselves, we are admitting our need for God. When God humbles us, He is trying to get our attention and save us from future disaster often caused by pride.

Ahab's attitude affected his descendants, but not in a positive manner. Although he "walked meekly" because of the prophet's stern warning, scripture does not indicate that he repented. In fact, he is called one of the most wicked kings who ever lived (1 Kings 21:25). Ahab was content to simply live out his remaining days apparently unconcerned how his actions would affect generations to come (see 1 Kings 21:29; 2 Kings 9:7; 21:13).

Jose, on the other hand, willingly chose to humble himself before the Lord by bearing the consequences for his previous wrongdoings. His repentant spirit positively affected his family. The lower he went, the higher God raised him. The Lord has blessed him with a devoted wife, four children, and a fruitful ministry.

What parent doesn't want his children to succeed? God's path to the pinnacle of promotion is paved with humility. It is the only road that lifts a person up while he is going down. If we lead the way, both we and our descendants will find ourselves seated at the Captain's table. And that, in God's eyes, is the highest level of achievement.

QUESTIONS THAT GROW

- What unfinished business do you need to complete so your descendants can experience God's blessing? How willing are you to face possible consequences for past wrongdoings?
- Paul said we should honor other people above ourselves (Romans 12:10) and we

should consider other people better than ourselves (Philippians 2:3). How easy or difficult is this for you to do? What makes it so difficult?

- If you are easily swayed by man's standard of promotion, what can you do to remain humble before God and man?

Chapter 17

HEEDING THE WARNING

*"Son of man, what is this proverb
you have in the land of Israel:
'The days go by and every vision
comes to nothing'?"*
EZEKIEL 12:22

The South Fork Dam in Johnstown, Pennsylvania, was one of the largest earthen dams in the world. Owned and maintained by some of the richest and most powerful men in America, it withstood the challenge of high water levels for years. As ownership of the seventy-two-foot-high dam changed hands, the structure slowly deteriorated. Any repairs were made carelessly and without the advice of experts. Over the years, workers cautioned that the dam could not withstand a major flood, but the warnings went unheeded. One article stated, "People wondered and asked why the dam was not strengthened, as it certainly had become weak, but nothing was done, and by and by, they talked less and less about it."[18]

On May 30, 1889, a storm hit Johnstown and the lake began to rise at an alarming rate—almost an inch every ten minutes. Workers tried feverishly to create another outlet to release the rush of water, but they couldn't keep up with the rapid pace at which the lake was rising. By midafternoon the depth and pressure of the water caused the bulging dam to crack and burst, and millions of tons of water, seventy to seventy-five feet high, surged

18. Information taken from the National Park Service visitors' guide for the Johnstown Flood National Memorial—Reading 2, www.nps.gov.

through the town at forty miles an hour. In less than an hour, Johnstown was engulfed in water, and more than 2,200 people lost their lives.[19]

The townspeople had been duly warned; but because the dam had stood for years, they ignored the warnings and assumed they were safe. What a costly, regrettable lesson.

The Israelites were also facing a serious flood—not one of water, but an invasion of their enemy, the Babylonians, who would take them into exile as captives. For years the Lord had spoken through the prophets—Isaiah, Jeremiah, Micah, Habakkuk, and Ezekiel—cautioning the Israelites of what was to come. Year after year, warning after warning, vision after vision, the prophets spoke and the people yawned. In fact, the Israelites had heard so many prophetic warnings about their imminent captivity, they began to flippantly recite a proverb: "The days go by and every vision comes to nothing."

Paremiologists—people who collect and study proverbs—say that the origins of most adages remain anonymous. However, all proverbs began at one time as memorable statements that caught on and were quoted by the people. The one God cited in Ezekiel 12:22 may not be traced to a specific person, but it does indicate the condition of the heart of the people—*apathetic*. Perhaps one day a

19. Ibid.

couple of people talked about how many times the prophets had shared a word from the Lord, saying something like: "Have you noticed how often the prophets have given us warnings, but nothing bad has happened? The days go by and every vision comes to nothing!" Maybe the people were in denial, convincing themselves that if a prophecy wasn't fulfilled, they had no need to worry about future devastation. Someone apparently repeated the saying to someone else, and soon it spread throughout the land of Israel. It's not vital to know where the saying originated. What is important is that the people believed it for years, and it led to their demise.

Even the prophet Isaiah, who lived years before Ezekiel, met opposition from the people. "See no more visions!" they cried. "Stop confronting us with the Holy One of Israel!" (Isaiah 30:10–11). God cautioned that one day their dam of human security would burst. "Because you have rejected this message, relied on oppression and depended on deceit, this sin will become for you like a high wall, cracked and bulging, that collapses suddenly, in an instant" (Isaiah 30:12–13). But the people threw caution to the wind and convinced themselves, "The vision he sees is for many years from now, and he prophesies about the distant future" (Ezekiel 12:27). *The days go by and every vision comes to nothing.*

God finally had enough. He was going to put their oft-repeated saying out of commission. "I am going to put an end to this proverb," He said. " 'They will no longer quote it in Israel.' Say to them, 'The days are near when every vision will be fulfilled'" (Ezekiel 12:23). What a rude awakening when that fateful day of captivity finally came. Did the people say, "We should have listened! We never should have quoted that proverb! If only we had another chance!"? We don't know for certain what they said, but we do know that everything God said came to pass.

Warnings about the future aren't exclusive to the Old Testament. The New Testament also contains numerous cautions for us, many of them given by Jesus Himself. He made it clear that no one knows the day nor the hour when He will return (see Matthew 24:36). However, we can recognize the seasonal changes. When the disciples asked Him about signs indicating the end of the age, Jesus told them to expect an increase and greater frequency of wars, rumors of wars, famines, earthquakes, persecution, false prophets, wickedness, and love that grows cold (see Matthew 24:3–12). The closer we come to the imminent return of the Lord, the higher the "water level of terrible times" (see 2 Timothy 3:1–4).

When the Lord gives a warning, He also offers a solution.

"*Keep watch*, because you do not know on what day your Lord will come" (Matthew 24:42, emphasis added; see also Matthew 25:13).

"*Watch and pray* so that you will not fall into temptation" (Matthew 26:41, emphasis added; see also Mark 14:38).

"*Watch out* that no one deceives you" (Mark 13:5, emphasis added; see also Luke 21:8).

"*Watch* your life and doctrine closely" (1 Timothy 4:16, emphasis added).

"*Watch out* that you do not lose what we have worked for" (2 John 1:8, emphasis added).

"*Be on guard! Be alert!* You do not know when that time will come" (Mark 13:33, emphasis added).

"Let us not be like others, who are asleep, but *let us be awake and sober*" (1 Thessalonians 5:6, emphasis added; see also 1 Peter 5:8).

It doesn't take much to recognize the signs of the Lord's imminent return. The dam is bulging and the rain clouds are overhead. If we live every day with the expectancy that it could be today, we will not be caught off guard. In fact, the last words of Jesus are a forewarning recorded in the prophetic book of Revelation: "Yes, I am coming soon" (Revelation 22:20). His words could be fulfilled at any time. Are you ready?

"Amen. Come, Lord Jesus!"

- What causes people to become apathetic when they are given a warning? What warnings have you been given that you have ignored?
- Some people don't want the Lord to come anytime soon because they are enjoying life too much. What is your attitude about the return of Jesus?
- What do the words "watch" and "be alert" mean to you? How can you become more watchful and alert?
- If you were a modern-day prophet, what warnings would you give people today? How do you think they would accept your words? If they ignored you, would you continue to warn them?

Chapter 18

REALITY CHECK

"What are you doing here?"
1 Kings 19:9

What a story! Elijah had just experienced a tremendous victory on Mount Carmel with a God-versus-Baal competition. God won. Elijah then prayed the severe drought would end. It did. You would think nothing could bring Elijah down from his victorious high. But something else happened. It took just one threat from Queen Jezebel to send Elijah running.

He had shown no fear on Mount Carmel when he faced hundreds of prophets of Baal; but the intimidation of one wicked queen sent him running to cower in the solitude of Mount Sinai. Have you noticed how Satan uses fear, intimidation, and doubt to suck the joy out of our mountaintop victories? When that happens, we can remain defeated, or we can learn and grow. What did Elijah learn from his experience?

He learned *running will get you nowhere*. He traveled around one hundred miles to go to a place where God didn't send him. Although an angel provided food and water for him en route, there is no indication that God instructed Elijah to take this trip. Sometimes the Lord lets us go out of our way just so we can learn a lesson—often the hard way.

Changing location or circumstances won't change us. Having a different husband or wife won't make us better spouses. Switching jobs won't make us better employees. Changing churches won't make us better parishioners. Soon we will discover the grass is never greener on the other side of the desert.

Instead of asking God to change everything and everyone else, perhaps we should ask Him to change us first. Then as we change, the perception we have of our circumstances will be different and our reactions might be a little less radical.

Elijah learned *negativity can cloud reality*. Why Mount Sinai? Maybe Elijah wanted a reenactment of Moses' experience when he met with God in the same location (see Exodus 19–20). But what would an exhausting trip to Mount Sinai give him that an astounding miracle on Mount Carmel did not?

To help Elijah face the reality of his circumstances, God challenged him when He asked, "What are you doing here?" It would be interesting to hear the inflection in God's voice. Did He ask, "What are *you* doing here?"—emphasizing Elijah's identity (anointed prophet)? Or "What are you *doing* here?"—emphasizing his actions (sulking and hiding)? Or did He ask, "What are you doing *here*?"—emphasizing the location (a place where God didn't tell him to go)?

Elijah's response to God's question was expressed from a bleak perspective: "I have been very zealous for the LORD God Almighty. The Israelites have rejected your covenant, broken down your altars, and put your prophets to death with the sword. I am the only one left, and now they are trying to kill me too" (1 Kings 19:10, 14). Most of what Elijah said was true. He was indeed zealous; the Israelites had rejected God's covenant, and they had broken down the altars and killed God's prophets. But Elijah was certainly not the only one left, and God gently reminded him he wasn't alone.

God never takes negativity for an answer. He knows pessimism can distort reality. Despair looks downward. Hope looks upward. The psalmist expressed the power in this truth when he said, "I lift up my eyes to the mountains—where does my help come from? My help comes from the LORD" (Psalm 121:1–2).

People who live on the negative side of life often find it easier to fall prey to discouragement, and sometimes even depression. If Satan can skew our perception, we will convince ourselves, as Elijah did, that we are alone and life has lost its meaning. If we allow ourselves to be swallowed up in our circumstances, we are more apt to resign, give up, walk away, or settle to live in a depressed state of mind. The best way to counter Satan's scheme is to allow the Lord to lift our heads above the cloud of our circumstances. He does that with His reality check: "What are you doing here?"

Elijah learned *obedience is healthy*. He was practically paralyzed by his own misconceptions. If he could just stay on Mount Sinai, he could die alone. But it wasn't God's will and it wasn't God's time. After asking the question twice and getting the same response, the Lord used a healthy maneuver. He moved Elijah into action:

- God sent him back the way he came (1 Kings 19:15). It was another trek of one hundred miles through the desert, but this time Elijah traveled with permission and power from God to carry on.
- Elijah was instructed to anoint, anoint, anoint (1 Kings 19:15–17). He may have felt drained, but God filled him with fresh hope, new energy, and clear vision. In turn, he was able to pour into the lives of Hazael, Jehu, and Elisha.
- He was assigned a mentee (1 Kings 19:19–21). Elijah assumed his ministry had lost effectiveness. In fact, he didn't just want to quit. He wanted to die. But God had other plans. He raised up a replacement, and a model mentoring relationship was established between Elijah and Elisha.
- God urged him on with the facts (1 Kings

19:18). Truth is liberating. When Elijah
bemoaned he was "the only one left," God
reminded him of seven thousand others still
in the ranks. It was the reality check Elijah
needed to start moving.

If Elijah had remained on Mount Sinai, he could
have died a quiet, peaceful death—alone. Who
could blame him? By the time he took his desert
detour, he had already done far more for God
than the average person. But his reality check was
discovering that God determines when the mission
is accomplished.

In the end, the man who sought solitude on
Sinai went out in a blaze of glory (2 Kings 2:11).
Way to go, Elijah!

Questions That Grow

- Where is your Mount Carmel? List
  significant victories you've experienced.
  What have you forgotten?
- Who/what is your Jezebel? How do you
  handle fear and intimidation? What can you
  do differently when it comes to facing fear?
- What are you doing "here"? Ask yourself
  that question using the three different word
  emphases—*you* (your identity), *doing* (your

actions or response), *here* (your present location). What needs to change to bring your concept of yourself, your actions, or your present location in alignment with God's plan for you?

- How do you think Elijah's journey *to* Mount Sinai differed from his journey *from* Mount Sinai? If God sent you back the way you came, what unfinished business would He ask you to complete?

- What value in your life can be poured into others? Name three people whom you will start pouring into. Who is your Elisha?

Chapter 19

THE BLAME GAME

"Where are you?"
GENESIS 3:9

Asked by God of Adam

My friend and I were playing in his backyard. We had found a large stick and were throwing it like a spear. "We need a target," he said as he surveyed the yard, looking for something to attack. Suddenly, the window on the garage door caught his attention. "Watch this," he said as he thrust the "spear" toward the window. Bull's-eye! He hit the target and the window remained intact. "Let me try," I said, picking up the stick and finding my best stance for spear throwing. I pitched it toward the window and successfully hit the target. Remarkably, the window didn't break. We were really on to something.

Whoever said "third time's the charm" probably wasn't talking about throwing sticks at windows. But we proved him correct that day. My friend grabbed the spear and, mustering all his strength, lunged toward the target. The glass shattered and we scattered. Tearing out of the yard, I heard his grandmother yell from the house, "David, just wait until your father gets home!"

My little eight-year-old legs ran home as fast as they could, and I made a beeline for my bedroom. I hid, waiting for the phone to ring—an indication David's grandma was reporting the misdeed to my parents. David ran, knowing his stern father would soon be home from work. I had already prepared my line of defense—"I didn't break the window. David did."

Why do we hide when we've done something wrong? Perhaps we think if we disappear, so will the transgression. Maybe we're afraid of the consequences, or we're concerned about what other people will think. Adam and Eve quickly learned it is impossible to hide from God. Once He pulled the truth from them, the blame game wouldn't work.

The Lord had been very explicit in His instructions to Adam: "You are free to eat from any tree in the garden; but you must not eat from the tree of the knowledge of good and evil, for when you eat from it you will surely die" (Genesis 2:16–17). Since God gave these orders to Adam before Eve was created, she received the instructions secondhand through Adam, not directly from God. Regardless of how each of them received the instructions, they both knew where the line was drawn, and they both chose to cross it by yielding to temptation.

Satan poses questions to create doubt. God asks questions to evoke truth. The very first question recorded in scripture was asked by Satan of the woman: "Did God really say, 'You must not eat from any tree in the garden'?" (Genesis 3:1). The very first questions the Lord asked were directed to the man, "Where are you? . . . Who told you that you were naked? Have you eaten from the tree that I commanded you not to eat from?" (Genesis 3:9, 11). Let the blame game begin.

Adam blamed God and Eve: "The woman you put here with me—she gave me some fruit from the tree, and I ate it" (Genesis 3:12). Eve blamed the devil: "The serpent deceived me, and I ate" (Genesis 3:13). God was unmoved by the accusations, and all three players—Adam, Eve, and the serpent—suffered the consequences.

I vaguely remember my friend David reporting later that his dad corrected him in an appropriate but very effective manner. No more spear throwing occurred after that incident. David learned his lesson. He never knew I was prepared to throw him under the bus to save my own skin.

I, on the other hand, faced no consequences. Unfortunately, I learned if I did something wrong, I could cover my transgression with "fig leaves." It wasn't until I was in college that God finally taught me the significance of nakedness.

The class was Personal Evangelism and the professor assigned us a book to read. We had an entire semester to read, and the assignment would count for half our grade. Like a typical college student, I procrastinated. The day before the exam, I skimmed through the book, reading short excerpts here and there. Then I designed my fig leaf garment by justifying that technically I *did* read the book. It all depended on how one defined "read."

The day of the exam, I stared at the first page of the test with the question, "Did you read the book in its entirety—yes or no?" Without hesitation, I checked "yes" and proceeded to complete the exam. I aced the class and went on to graduate and enter full-time ministry. My, those fig leaves fit well and felt extremely comfortable.

A few years later God began to tug at my fig leaves and at my heart. "You cheated on that exam," He whispered. All my reasoning and justifying carried no weight with God. My clothing completely unraveled when He warned, "If you don't make this right, your spiritual growth will stop right here." God didn't have to tell me twice. I contacted the professor and confessed. He graciously forgave me, and I more than made up for my misdeed. By the way, fig leaves become very itchy after a while.

Taking responsibility for our actions is imperative for character development and spiritual maturity (read Ephesians 4:22–5:10). God gave Adam and Eve instructions and a choice. He does the same with us. What we choose determines our future. God is not responsible for our growth. We are.

Solomon said, "God will bring every deed into judgment, including every hidden thing, whether it is good or evil" (Ecclesiastes 12:14). Jesus reiterated this truth when He told His disciples, "There is nothing hidden that will not be disclosed, and nothing concealed that will not be known or brought out into the open" (Luke 8:17).

Whether we are running from a broken window or from cheating on an exam, nothing is more comfortable than being naked before God. His warm embrace of love and forgiveness is all the covering we need.

QUESTIONS THAT GROW

- How do you hide from God? When God calls and you emerge from hiding, how does He respond to you? How do you respond to Him?

- What do you do when your self-made covering of fig leaves becomes itchy? What is God trying to tell you when your life becomes uncomfortable because you're hiding?

- Are you running from any broken windows that may be partly your own fault? Although you may not be able to repair the windows, what do you need to do to repair shattered relationships?

Chapter 20

WHAT'S BIGGER THAN GOD?

*"Who is this that obscures my plans
with words without knowledge?"*
Job 38:2

"What's bigger than Jesus?" my five-year-old granddaughter asked me one day, her big brown eyes dancing with amused challenge. Then she added, "And you can't say 'nothing.'" I realized this was more about matching wits than it was childish curiosity. I thought a minute and replied, "His shadow." She mulled this over for a bit and then asked, "Okay. Then who's *smarter* than Jesus? And you can't say 'nobody.'" She got me. I was stumped.

No doubt Job and his friends were also stumped when God came on the scene and peppered them with questions. God never asks a question to which He doesn't know the answer. The Lord's questions are intended to create awareness, evoke thought, and help a person face reality.

God's appearance couldn't have been better timed. Job was at the tail end of the most horrendous trial any human could face—loss of his children, his possessions, and his health. His "comforters" weren't much help either, as they tried to figure out what sin he had committed to deserve such a crisis.

"Brace yourself like a man," God said. "I will question you, and you shall answer me" (Job 38:3). Then He proceeded to pose more than seventy questions, including the following:

- "Have you ever given orders to the morning, or shown the dawn its place?" (Job 38:12)
- "Have you comprehended the vast expanses of the earth? Tell me, if you know all this." (Job 38:18)
- "Have you entered the storehouses of the snow or seen the storehouses of the hail, which I reserve for times of trouble, for days of war and battle?" (Job 38:22–23)
- "Do you give the horse his strength or clothe his neck with a flowing mane?" (Job 39:19)

Then came the stinger, shocking Job into silence: "Will the one who contends with the Almighty correct him? Let him who accuses God answer him!" (Job 40:2). In the midst of the barrage of queries, Job timidly responded, "I am unworthy— how can I reply to you? I put my hand over my mouth" (Job 40:4).

Ironically, Job had had no problem earlier speaking up to his friends when they sermonized and preached and evaluated his dilemma (see Job 7:11; 13:13). At one point he even boldly declared, "I desire to speak to the Almighty and to argue my case with God" (Job 13:3). God heard and showed up. Job now had his chance to "argue his case," but he was too stunned to speak.

Notice God didn't offer Job sympathy, nor

did He harshly correct him for expressing his frustrations. But He did put Job and his friends in their place by putting everything into perspective. The more the Lord revealed His greatness, the more diminutive these men appeared.

Theologian and Christian apologist Timothy Keller tells of a life-changing experience he had in school as a result of something his teacher said.

> *"Let's assume the distance between the earth and the sun (92 million miles) was reduced to the thickness of a sheet of paper. If that is the case, then the distance between the earth and the nearest star would be a stack of papers 70 feet high. And the diameter of the galaxy would be a stack of papers 310 miles high."* The teacher continued, *"The galaxy is just a speck of dust in the universe, yet Jesus holds the universe together by the word of his power."* Finally, the teacher asked, *"Now, is this the kind of person you ask to be your assistant— or to rule your life?"* (from Keller's sermon *"The Gospel and Yourself"*)

If we could truly grasp the enormity of God and His power, we just might relinquish more control to Him and assume less for ourselves. Then life's storms would be seen from a different perspective.

Notice where God was when He spoke. He answered Job "out of the storm" (Job 38:1; 40:6), indicating He was in the *midst* of the storm. The Lord could have thundered directly from heaven. Instead He revealed Himself as the Master over nature. Job was in a storm, and God was right there with him.

Matthew records two instances when Jesus intentionally sent the disciples into storms. The first account is found in Matthew 8:23–27. After the disciples entered the boat, a storm came up unexpectedly and they nearly drowned. Meanwhile, Jesus slept soundly while the disciples panicked. When they woke Him, He commented about their little faith and asked why they were so afraid. Then He simply spoke to nature and the storm stopped. The disciples' response was: "What kind of man is this? Even the winds and the waves obey him!" (Matthew 8:27).

The second narrative is related in Matthew 14:22–33. After feeding the crowd of five thousand, Jesus went off to pray while the disciples sailed through high winds and waves totally alone—or so they thought. Sometime between 3:00 a.m. and 6:00 a.m., Jesus showed up doing what no human could possibly do—He walked on the water toward their boat. Peter climbed out of the boat and made an attempt to walk on the water toward

Jesus. Nearly drowning, Peter called for help and Jesus caught him. They both climbed into the boat and the wind died down immediately. This time the disciples responded not with a question but with a declaration: "Truly you are the Son of God" (Matthew 14:33). It took a storm for them to realize who Jesus Christ really was.

Life's storms are never easy, and God doesn't intend for them to be, because He knows that every storm serves a purpose—and every storm comes to an end. When Job's tempest finally subsided, he confessed, "My ears had heard of you but now my eyes have seen you" (Job 42:5). Catching a fresh glimpse of the Almighty was worth it all.

Sometimes the Lord takes a calm, restful role while our boat rocks perilously. Other times He appears out of nowhere, controlling the storm with His feet. And occasionally He speaks to us out of the midst of the tempest. Regardless of where He appears, the Lord will always show up if our focus remains on Him. It's always safer to be in the midst of a storm with Him than to dwell in the calm without Him.

QUESTIONS THAT GROW

- How have you found God in the midst of challenging circumstances? How long did

it take for you to recognize Him? What
difference did it make once you saw how
close He was to you?

- How do you discern between God's wise
counsel and man's feeble opinion? Which
one carries more influence with you? How
can you focus more clearly on God's voice?
- What are times when the Lord has called
you to "come out of the boat" and walk
toward Him? What happened when you
took your eyes off of Him and looked at your
circumstances instead?
- When are times you have treated God as an
assistant rather than a ruler? What needs to
change so He rules your life full-time?

Chapter 21

LEAVING A LEGACY

"Did I ever say. . .'Why have you not built me a house of cedar?'"
2 SAMUEL 7:7

Asked by God of David

King David was a unique individual. His fearless military exploits are amazing and his songs (psalms) are moving and soul-baring. He maintained his composure while in battle, but his emotions went wild as he penned his thoughts and sang them to God. He was a warrior by day and a musician by night. After years of great military victories, King David was finally enjoying rest from his enemies (2 Samuel 7:1). Now he had time to focus on matters that had been left untended, including providing a permanent place for the ark of God. He had built a beautiful house for himself. Why not build one for the Lord?

The ark of the covenant was built under the direction of Moses (see Exodus 25:10–22). It was the most significant piece of furniture the Israelites possessed because it represented the presence of the Lord. For centuries, the ark had been carried from place to place as the Israelites wandered in the desert. When they finally claimed their promised land, it was housed in a tent called the Tabernacle. Now that David was settled in a permanent home, he wanted to build a long-lasting dwelling place for the presence of the Lord.

Even Nathan the prophet agreed that David should move ahead with his plans, adding, "The

Lord is with you" (2 Samuel 7:3). However, God had other plans, and He made those plans known to Nathan, who in turn reported God's words to the king. *David was not to build a temple for the Lord. Instead, one of his offspring would become the designated builder.*

Have you ever been inspired to do something great for God but later learned He wasn't even in it? Not every good idea is God's idea. The Lord asked David, "Did I ever say. . .'Why have you not built me a house of cedar?'" (2 Samuel 7:7). David was a visionary and his idea was noble, but it wasn't from the Lord.

One visionary leader I know has created a safety net to avoid disastrous decisions. He has an agreement with the Lord that when he is struck with what might be considered a world-changing idea, he waits for two or three confirmations from the Lord. No confirmation? No action. He explains, "Sometimes it's the right thing but the wrong time. And sometimes it's just a momentary dream that should never reach reality." For David, it was the right thing but the wrong time *and* the wrong builder.

After Nathan cautioned him not to proceed with his building plans, David acknowledged the Lord's omniscience and sat down to converse with Him (see 2 Samuel 7:18). Sometimes just sitting with the Lord for a short time can accomplish more than hours of activity.

Several years ago I was in a quandary about a certain decision, so I hired a coach to help me create a plan and work through my next steps. During one of our conversations, she asked if I had ever considered starting a "mastermind group." I had never heard of such a thing and asked her to describe it.

A mastermind group, she explained, is made up of four to ten individuals who meet frequently to help each other work through current challenges and set goals. The expertise of each individual is pooled so everyone can get the most benefit from the group. I thought the idea was brilliant and immediately asked God to show me who I should include in such a group. God responded, "I am your Master and I have a mind." It was an invitation to sit with Him and pick His brain! How genius!

The next morning I officially began a mastermind group with the Master. I just sat with God and let Him speak to my heart. The experience was incredible. He spoke wisdom and insight in a few moments' time and I left our first meeting overwhelmed that He cared so deeply about the most trivial matters in my life. Over the years we have enjoyed countless sessions where I sit and He speaks. Sometimes I leave our meetings with a clear action plan. Other times I emerge with nothing to do. Sitting is sufficient. Obedience to do nothing can accomplish more for eternity than a flurry of temporary activity.

David showed a humble, obedient heart as he set aside his notoriety and surrendered his will to God. He knew he would never leave a legacy as the temple builder. Instead, he helped prepare the way so his son Solomon could step into the role.

Toward the end of his life, David presented Solomon with the plans for the temple inspired by God. He donated today's equivalent of billions of dollars' worth of gold and silver. Then David encouraged the people to step up and give toward the project he would never lift a finger to build. They responded by donating *tons* (literally!) of gold, silver, bronze, and iron (see 1 Chronicles 28–29).

David's final words emboldened Solomon to begin the task of building the temple: "Be strong and courageous, and do the work. Do not be afraid or discouraged, for the Lord God, my God, is with you. He will not fail you or forsake you until all the work for the service of the temple of the Lord is finished" (1 Chronicles 28:20).

That's a legacy Solomon could work with.

- Are you a visionary? What safety net have you put in place to avoid careless actions? How easy or difficult is it for you to release your plans?
- What ideas are in your planner now that God has not inspired? What do you need to hear from God as assurance that you should move forward? What if He tells you to stop?
- How often do you "sit" with God? If you could pick His brain, what would you want to learn?
- How would work in the church be affected if no one cared who received the credit? Why is recognition or acknowledgment so important to some people? How important is it to you?
- What are you doing to equip the next generation? What legacy will you leave?

Chapter 22

TAKING A STAND

*"What are you doing
down on your face?"*
JOSHUA 7:10

Aesop's fable "The Brave Mice" tells the story of a group of mice and their plan to conquer a menacing cat. An older mouse, thought to be very wise, suggested they hang a bell on the cat's neck as a warning of the cat's approach. When all the mice agreed, the old mouse asked, "Now which of you will hang this bell on the cat's neck?" The mice all scampered away to their holes. The moral: *Real bravery lies in deeds, not words.*[20]

Scampering into a hole is often easier than taking a stand against something harmful. However, the trade-off for avoidance is the spread of what could become toxic. God knows how to motivate us so we don't suffer the consequences of our own immobility.

The Israelites had just crossed the Jordan River, ready to claim the Promised Land. The only way they could reach their destination was to conquer the formidable city of Jericho. The Lord gave them an amazing victory as they watched the wall miraculously crumble (Joshua 6). He instructed Joshua and the Israelites to place all the plunder from Jericho in the Lord's treasury, keeping nothing for themselves (Joshua 6:18–19).

Their next conquest was the city of Ai. Spies

---

20. William J. Bennett, *The Book of Virtues* (New York: Simon & Schuster, 1993), 457.

assured Joshua that three thousand men could easily defeat this tiny town. However, the men of Ai set up an ambush and chased the Israelites into the stone quarries where they were struck down and killed. Joshua was devastated and the "hearts of the people melted in fear and became like water" (Joshua 7:5). In an act of contrition, Joshua fell facedown before the ark of the Lord, asking God why He brought them this far only to let them be conquered by a small town. The victory at Jericho would now be negated when the other countries heard about the Israelites' defeat.

Sometimes when we face challenging circumstances, God gently embraces us and softly whispers, "Shhhhh. Be at peace, My child. I'll take care of it." Other times, He grabs us by the collar and thrusts us into combat. This was Joshua's time to move. "Stand up!" God said. "What are you doing down on your face?" (Joshua 7:10). God's question was a call to action. Sin had entered the camp and an entire nation was in jeopardy.

In Joshua 7:11–12, we read how the Lord pronounced blame on Israel nine times. It was obvious who was at fault. "They" did it! But God wasn't finished—"I will not be with *you* anymore unless *you* destroy whatever among *you* is devoted to destruction" (Joshua 7:12, emphasis added). All of a sudden, it wasn't "they." It was "you," referring to

Joshua. Sin may have been brought into the camp by one person, but Joshua and the Israelites had to do something about it.

While Joshua was "down on his face," he asked God, "What then will *you* do for your own great name?" (Joshua 7:9, emphasis added). When God pulled Joshua to his feet, He intended for *Joshua* to do something. God won't do something for us if it means we will become weakened in the process. If Joshua was willing to tackle this situation, he would become a stronger, more effective leader.

Confronting people who have sinned or erred is not always easy, but it is crucial for the health and well-being of those who have been affected by the sin. Scripture offers this guiding principle for confrontation: *the range of the offense determines the extent of the correction.*

Consider these examples:

- *An individual.* In Matthew 18:15 Jesus instructed, "If your brother or sister sins, go and point out their fault, just between the two of you." If the sin is within the scope of two individuals, the initial correction must remain within that boundary. No one else should even be told about the situation until you have approached the other person. What a wonderful opportunity for quiet reconciliation. If the brother doesn't listen, then approach him again with a witness (Matthew 18:16). If he still refuses to listen, the last resort is to inform the leaders and let them deal with the issue.

- *A group.* Jesus harshly corrected the self-righteous religious leaders in the presence of the crowds (see Matthew 23). These teachers were blatant hypocrites, teaching one thing but doing the opposite (Matthew 23:3). Why did Jesus confront them publicly? Because the range of their offense affected a large number of people, and Jesus wanted the people to witness the correction. Those individuals we oversee and teach need to see us take a stand against false teaching or hypocrisy that can harm the body.

- *A church.* In the book of Acts we read about the birth of the church. Everyone was united and shared their possessions (Acts 4:32). Landowners sold property and gave the proceeds to the treasury. Ananias and Sapphira made a sale and gave an appearance of generosity. But secretly they withheld a portion for themselves. The Holy Spirit revealed this sin to Peter and he immediately confronted them. Because they had "lied to the Holy Spirit" (Acts

5:3), God brought judgment and both Ananias and Sapphira were struck dead. Why such severe consequences? Because the newly formed fellowship was in the baby stage. If the sin had not been dealt with at the inception of the church, it could have caused an infection that would have spread throughout the entire congregation. In the same way, we must remain sensitive to the Holy Spirit when dealing with sin, taking personal inventory to ensure our hearts are pure before approaching someone else regarding their sin. Then, under the Lord's direction, we can bring whatever correction is necessary to maintain spiritual health.

- *A nation.* Even after God gave specific instructions for the Israelites not to keep any plunder from Jericho for themselves, Achan's coveting heart got the best of him. One man's iniquity caused the death of soldiers and put an entire nation at risk. God could have revealed to Joshua who it was who committed the sin. Instead, the people assembled as Joshua called them tribe by tribe, clan by clan, and family by family. After Achan was revealed as the violator, he and his entire family and all of their possessions were destroyed (Joshua

7:25–26). The future of Israel was in jeopardy because one man disobeyed the instructions given to an entire nation. The scope of the offense was nationwide, and the confrontation remained within the same range.

Maybe it's time for us to get up, take a stand, and move into action by confronting, correcting, and reconciling. It's the one responsibility that, if delegated to someone else, will cost us the development of strength and character. That's too high a price to pay. What are *you* doing down on your face?

QUESTIONS THAT GROW

- What confrontation(s) are you avoiding that needs to happen? What are you afraid will happen if you do confront? What will happen if you don't?
- How can you tell when it's time to just pray and when it's time to act?
- In Matthew 18:17 we read how Jesus told the disciples to treat someone who refuses to reconcile. "Treat him as a pagan or tax collector." How did Jesus treat pagans and tax collectors?

- Why doesn't God deal as harshly today with those who cover their sin as He did with Ananias and Sapphira? What do you do when people seem to be getting away with their sin?

Chapter 23

THE FREEDOM OF BOUNDARIES

"What more could have been done for my vineyard than I have done for it? When I looked for good grapes, why did it yield only bad?"

ISAIAH 5:4

Several years ago I heard an evangelist share three things God cannot do: (1) He cannot lie; (2) He cannot fill a clenched fist; and (3) He cannot save a soul that does not want to be saved. Based on Isaiah 5:4, we may be able to add a fourth thing to the list: He cannot do more for His vineyard than He has already done.

The Lord was very devoted to the nation of Israel. He even wrote a love song for His beloved people, whom He referred to as a vineyard. He did everything possible to create fertile land that would produce a garden of delight (Isaiah 5:7). He built a watchtower (for protection), a winepress (for expected fruit), and borders (for protection from enemy invasions). Sadly, Israel didn't possess the same devotion to the Lord that He carried for them. God had invested time and effort so the Israelites could be blessed above all other nations. But when He examined the fruit of His labors, He found no good fruit (Isaiah 5:4). All that work and nothing to show for it. Israel remained indifferent to God's overtures of love.

Apathy carries consequences. "I will take away its hedge, and it will be destroyed. I will break down its wall, and it will be trampled" (Isaiah 5:5). In other words, God chose to remove Himself from the scene and allow the Israelites to have what they wanted all along—their own way by their own devices. God saw potential, but Israel remained indifferent.

The story of God and the vineyard of disappointment can be an important example for us. God's power may be limitless, but He works within certain limitations. He knows when to invest and when to release—when to pour in and when to pull away. It would benefit us to apply the same standard regarding our own relationships with people. If the Lord saw the necessity of drawing the line, He will enable us to do the same. He will create a safe space in which we can live and work.

Jesus honored the boundaries of His Father. "My Father is always at his work to this very day, and I too am working. . . . The Son can do nothing by himself; he can do only what he sees his Father doing, because whatever the Father does the Son also does" (John 5:17, 19).

The Gospel of Mark records the story of a certain ruler who approached Jesus and asked how he could inherit eternal life. Jesus told him to follow the commandments. The ruler responded that he had kept all of the commandments since his youth. Jesus then instructed him to sell everything he had, give it to the poor, and follow Him. The man walked away very sad because he had great wealth and didn't want to give it up (Mark 10:17–23). Jesus just watched him walk. He didn't chase him to renegotiate that he sell only 50 percent of his riches. He didn't try to coerce him with an easier option. Jesus had done all He could. Now it was up to the man to do all *he* could.

One mistake we often make is to pour our passion into passionless people. We see potential in others and are determined to help them reach goals they never set for themselves. The reality is, not everyone wants to move forward. Some people are simply content to remain the same and enjoy watching someone else work hard on their behalf.

As a young minister, I mistook my excitement to see others change as passion for God's work. Anyone who showed the least amount of potential had my attention. However, not everyone desires to reach their potential. Ministry was draining me dry, and I was a willing—and ignorant—participant. I couldn't understand why the Lord would call me to do work I didn't enjoy. The pitifully small amount of fruit just wasn't worth the effort.

God rescued me by establishing a boundary within which I could work. "I don't intend for you to help everybody," He gently instructed. (How freeing is that!) He continued, "Work within the safe zone I have created for you, and I will restore your joy for ministry." His cautionary words provided me with the perfect parameter that saved me from myself. The joy of working for the Lord soon returned, thanks to the hedge of protection around me. Now I recognize the difference between people who are exhausting and those who are energizing. I learned we can only do so much. If people don't want to change, they will choose to walk away. What more can we do?

The owner of a local apple orchard used to hire workers whose primary job was to cut down the plants growing at the base of the fruit trees. These plants are called "suckers." They grow quickly and look attractive, almost as if they're an important part of the orchard. However, suckers drain life from a tree. If these plants are not removed, the tree will bear less and less fruit. In time, the tree itself will have to be removed because the deadly growth has drained the tree of its ability to yield fruit.

Over the years, the Israelites allowed the "suckers" of apathy, idolatry, and rebellion to destroy their ability to generate produce pleasing in the eyes of the Lord. As a result, God removed the protective barriers and allowed the enemy to come in and drain Israel dry. What more could the Lord have done?

God's analogy of a vineyard is interesting. He knows the importance of enjoying the fruit of one's labors. Sometimes we need to just sit back and relish the sweet grapes in the vineyard where God has placed us to labor. He knows a glass of freshly squeezed juice is extremely revitalizing. Stay faithful to the Lord, work within His protective boundaries, and drink up. Cheers!

QUESTIONS THAT GROW

- What parameters do you need so your work for the Lord is energizing and not exhausting? How will you know you are working within God's protective boundaries?
- How do you recognize the fruit of your labors? When was the last time you enjoyed eating the fruit?
- If a "rich young ruler" type of person approached you, how easy would it be for you to let him walk away? What difference do you think it would have made if Jesus had renegotiated with him?
- How would you answer God's question, "What more could have been done for My vineyard?" What does His question give you permission to do?

Chapter 24

SHIFTING GEARS

*"Where have you come from,
and where are you going?"*
GENESIS 16:8

Asked by God of Hagar

The state of Tennessee has winding and hilly roads that make driving a little precarious. Truck runaway ramps are a common sight. Cautious drivers use the rearview mirror almost as much as they look through the windshield, because checking for what's behind helps a person determine the safest lane for moving forward. A semitruck barreling downhill behind you in your lane is a warning to change lanes and let the truck pass. Rearview mirrors can save lives!

The Lord's question to Hagar caused her to look through both the rearview mirror and the windshield. God didn't analyze *why*. He was interested in *where*: *Where have you come from and where are you going?* When Hagar admitted she had run from her abusive mistress, the Lord instructed her to return and submit to the very one from whom she was running.

Years earlier, God had promised Abram that he would father a son and his offspring would number more than he could count (Genesis 15:1). Since Sarai was barren, she and Abram decided to take things into their own hands and give God a little help. Sarai offered her Egyptian servant, Hagar, to Abram as a secondary wife who would bear his child. Sarai reasoned that as long as Abram was the father, it didn't matter who gave birth to the son. When Hagar learned she was pregnant, Sarai regretted her decision. Hagar may have been the "secondary" wife, but she could bear children and Sarai could not. Hagar held this over her mistress's head and began to despise her. Sarai retaliated by mistreating Hagar until she ran away into the desert (Genesis 16:4–6).

Hagar's name means "flight." By nature, she was a runner. Perhaps her mother was a runner, too, which may be how she got her name. People on the run tend to make anxious decisions because they're running from something in their past rather than running toward their future. It's easy to run. But the easy way out isn't always the best way. No matter where Hagar might go, she would still be the same Hagar. Changing her location wouldn't change her as a person. Neither would ignoring her unpleasant circumstance make it go away. God put the brakes on the runner so she could stop and face her situation.

Aren't you glad God stops us in our tracks before we follow through with rash decisions that could have potentially harmful results? Sometimes we just need to be saved from ourselves.

"Where have you come from, and where are you going?" the Lord asked. Notice that Hagar answered only part of the question, stating she was running from her mistress. Did she even know where she was going? We are given a clue that since she was on the "road to Shur," she may have been headed back to Egypt. God sent her back to deliver—and to be delivered from her tendency to run.

When God instructs us to go back and rectify a situation, He always empowers us with hope and encouragement. Before Hagar returned to face her situation, the Lord gave the name for her unborn son—Ishmael, which means "God hears." This encounter with the Lord was memorialized through her son. Every time Hagar looked at Ishmael she could remember that God hears in the most desperate hour. She responded by giving the Lord a new name: *the One who sees me* (Genesis 16:13–14). God heard. God saw. Now she could go back and face anything.

It's always easy to wait for the other person to make the first move, isn't it? However, God doesn't always work that way. He wants us to see our own need for change before we focus on how we think the other person should change. God knew Hagar was not completely innocent. He had heard and seen everything. He also knew Hagar's healing would come if she returned to face the one she had offended. Scripture doesn't indicate that God ever corrected Sarai for abusing Hagar. Instead, the victimized slave girl set the standard.

Submission means to accept something we have resisted or opposed. It's not easy to defer to someone we don't respect. It's also difficult to show respect to someone we think doesn't deserve it.

A young man argued constantly with his alcoholic father. The son admitted he had zero respect for him because of his lifestyle. One day, God showed the young man that even if he couldn't respect his father as a person, he needed to at least respect his father's position. When the son embraced this truth, his attitude began to change— and so did the dad's. Although the drinking didn't stop completely, the arguing ceased and the two men slowly rebuilt the relationship that had deteriorated.

Hagar returned, not as the secondary wife, but as Sarai's servant, whom she served for thirteen more years. Because of her obedience, her next steps came from a humble heart, not from a running spirit.

No matter how dark or difficult our situation may seem, a fresh revelation of God can shed a whole new light on our circumstance. Hagar may have been stranded in the desert, but God saw! And she saw that God saw. That's all that mattered.

Are you being chased by unfinished business from your past? Maybe God is sending you back to tie up loose ends. Every runner knows he can't run well with loose laces. Paul admonished, "Throw off everything that hinders and the sin that so easily entangles. And let us run with perseverance the race marked out for us, fixing our eyes on Jesus, the pioneer and perfecter of faith" (Hebrews 12:1–2).

Remember, it's not a chase. It's a race.

Questions That Grow

- What is your immediate response when you are treated unfairly? How quickly do you run? How willing are you to stay put and be a peacemaker?
- The windshield on a car is many times larger than the rearview mirror. What applications can be made from this analogy? Do you spend more time looking back or looking forward?
- If God told you today to "go back," what character quality would He be developing in you? Where would you "go back" to?
- What characteristic about God can you learn from your most recent challenging circumstance? What is a new name you can give Him based on what you learned from this situation?
- What is chasing you from your past? How can you turn the chase into a race?

Chapter 25

LETTING GOD BE GOD

*"Should I not have concern
for the great city of Nineveh?"*
JONAH 4:11

Asked by God of Jonah

Several years ago a man who claimed to be a Christian defrauded another person. I became angry and fervently prayed, "God, You deal with him. He needs to suffer for what he's done." To my consternation, the man seemed to prosper and enjoy God's blessings rather than experience His wrath.

Around a year later, the man fell into hard times. The Lord impressed me to pray for him again. This time I wept as I prayed for God to have mercy on him. Within a short time, the man repented and paid restitution to the person he had offended the year before. I was amazed at how quickly God worked. "Why didn't You answer my prayer a year ago?" I asked the Lord. He responded, "Because I was waiting for you to change first." My merciless heart was being changed by a merciful God.

Jonah the prophet also struggled with a merciless heart toward people he felt deserved retribution. When God called him to Nineveh to preach repentance, He was sending him into enemy territory. As far as Jonah was concerned, the Ninevites did not deserve forgiveness. They deserved punishment. And he had good reason to feel that way.

Nineveh was the capital of Assyria, a fierce enemy of the Jews. Jonah, a Jewish prophet, had witnessed how the ruthless and barbaric Assyrians had brutalized his people. God's instruction for him to go to Nineveh was a call to the center of terrorism, captivity, bondage, and death. The Assyrians had massacred enemy soldiers, beheaded enemy kings, and enslaved helpless women. The Jews experienced mass deportations at the hands of the Assyrians. It wasn't unusual for them to publicly humiliate the enemy king by putting a ring in his nose and pulling him along like a dog on a leash. Those not deported were subject to humiliation and heavy taxes under the cruel hand of these barbarians. No wonder Jonah ran the other way.

When it comes to sin, God doesn't turn a blind eye. Instead, He sees everything through the scope of love. The Lord wanted to demonstrate His character by offering mercy before judgment, and He intended to use Jonah as a vessel of His compassion and love. Jonah refused and boarded a boat headed in the opposite direction. As a result of his disobedience, God sent a severe storm that terrified the most seasoned sailors on the ship.

Jonah knew he was the cause of the storm and told the sailors to throw him overboard so they wouldn't suffer for his disobedience. God then sent a huge fish to swallow Jonah, where he remained for three days as he called for mercy. The Lord heard his plea and commanded the fish to hurl Jonah out of his mouth. The prophet had learned his lesson. Now he was ready to obey and go to Assyria.

Jonah's message to the Ninevites was simple: "Forty more days and Nineveh will be overthrown" (Jonah 3:4). His warning was enough to move the king into action. He called the entire city (including animals) to a total fast and urged the people to call urgently upon the Lord and give up their evil, violent ways (see Jonah 3:8). The prophet's message worked!

Paul says in Romans 2:4 that God's kindness leads us to repentance. Before He brings judgment, the Lord always gives opportunity for people to repent. The kindest thing Jonah could have done for the Ninevites was to offer them a chance to repent.

In Proverbs 25:21–22, we read, "If your enemy is hungry, give him food to eat; if he is thirsty, give him water to drink. In doing this, you will heap burning coals on his head." As a young Christian, I interpreted this scripture as permission to add to my enemy's misery. By heaping "hot coals" on my adversary's head, I could increase the heat of his punishment in hell. Sadly, I received much ignorant gratification from that sordid thought. Maybe Jonah had the same mind-set as mine.

A more accurate interpretation of the passage in Proverbs 25 stems from an ancient custom of repentance. If a person committed a wrongdoing, he would carry a pan of hot coals on his head to show his sorrow. So when we "heap hot coals" on our enemy's head, we are helping lead him to repentance. Scripture instructs us to show kindness to our enemy and to encourage penitence, not punishment.

The book of Jonah has a very sad ending. After delivering the message of repentance, Jonah left the city and sat down to watch what he hoped would be divine annihilation. The burning sun beat down on his head, and God provided a vine that grew quickly and mercifully offered him a bit of shelter. However, the next morning, the Lord allowed a worm to destroy the vine, leaving Jonah unprotected. He mourned over the lost vine more than he did over the lost city.

As Jonah sat on the outskirts of Nineveh, he opined, "I knew that you are a gracious and compassionate God, slow to anger and abounding in love, a God who relents from sending calamity. Now, LORD, take away my life, for it is better for me to die than to live" (Jonah 4:2–3). He might as well have said, "God, I don't like the way You are. I wish You weren't so merciful and compassionate. I'd rather die than see my enemy repent." Apparently Jonah forgot how the Lord had shown him compassion by delivering him from the belly of the fish.

In the end, the Lord couldn't help but be

concerned for the great city of Nineveh, no matter how wicked the people had been. It's who He is, and He cannot contradict His own character. Thank God for that!

QUESTIONS THAT GROW

- When do you find it difficult to show mercy? How has God shown mercy to you?
- Who is your adversary? What acts of kindness can you show to "heap coals of fire" in an effort to lead that person to repentance?
- Ephesians 6:12 states, "Our struggle is not against flesh and blood, but against the rulers. . .authorities. . .powers of this dark world and against the spiritual forces of evil in the heavenly realms." How does this scripture change a person's perspective regarding the true identity of his enemy?
- If you could change something about God, what would you change? What's keeping you from changing yourself so you can be aligned with His character instead of expecting Him to change to acquiesce to yours?

ABOUT THE AUTHOR

Mary Selzer is an inspirational speaker, Bible teacher, and professional coach who works with executives, leaders, and teams. Her passion is to inspire people to love and live by God's Word. She has won two writing awards for her devotionals, and in 2015 she published *Wait a Minute—Thirty Devotionals Inspired by Life's Breath-Catching Moments.* Mary and her husband live in St. Clair Shores, Michigan. Visit Mary's website at www.coachingforward.net.

INDEX

A Complete List of All the Questions God Asked

If her father had spit in her face, would she not have
    been in disgrace for seven days? Numbers 12:14 . . . . .Moses
How long will these people treat me with contempt?
    Numbers 14:11 . . . . .Moses
How long will they refuse to believe in me, in spite
    of all the miraculous signs I have performed among
    them? Numbers 14:11 NIV 1984 . . . . .Moses
How long will this wicked community
    grumble against me? Numbers 14:27 . . . . .Moses and Aaron
Who are these men with you? Numbers 22:9 . . . . . . .Balaam
Are the trees people, that you should
    besiege them? Deuteronomy 20:19 . . . . Israel
Have I not commanded you? Joshua 1:9 . . . . Joshua
What are you doing down on your face? Joshua 7:10 . . .Joshua
When the Egyptians, the Amorites, the Ammonites,
    the Philistines, the Sidonians, the Amalekites,
    and the Maonites oppressed you and you cried to
    me for help, did I not save you from their hands?
    Judges 10:11–12 (see Genesis 12) . . . . .Israelites
Did I not clearly reveal myself to your ancestor's
    family when they were in Egypt under Pharaoh?
    1 Samuel 2:27 . . . . Eli
Why do you scorn my sacrifice and offering that
    I prescribed for my dwelling? 1 Samuel 2:29 . . . . Eli
Why do you honor your sons more than me by
    fattening yourselves on the choice parts of every
    offering made by my people Israel? 1 Samuel 2:29 . . . . . Eli
How long will you mourn for Saul, since I have
    rejected him as king over Israel? 1 Samuel 16:1 . . . . . Samuel
Are you the one to build me a house to
    dwell in? 2 Samuel 7:5 . . . . David (via Nathan)
Wherever I have moved with all the Israelites,
    did I ever say to any of their rulers whom I
    commanded to shepherd my people Israel. . .
    Why have you not built me a house of cedar?
    2 Samuel 7:7; 1 Chronicles 17:6 . . . . David
What are you doing here, Elijah? 1 Kings 19:9, 13 . . . . . Elijah
Have you noticed how Ahab has humbled
    himself? 1 Kings 21:29 . . . . Elijah

What is the way to the abode of light? Job 38:19 . . . . Job
And where does darkness reside? Job 38:19 . . . . Job
Can you take them to their places? Job 38:20 . . . . Job
Do you know the paths to their dwellings? Job 38:20 . . . . Job
Have you entered the storehouses of the snow or
   seen the storehouses of the hail, which I reserve
   for times of trouble, for days of war and battle?
   Job 38:22–23 . . . . Job
What is the way to the place where the lightning
   is dispersed, or the place where the east winds are
   scattered over the earth? Job 38:24 . . . . Job
Who cuts a channel for the torrents of rain,
   a path for the thunderstorm, to water a land
   where no one lives, an uninhabited desert,
   to satisfy a desolate wasteland and make it
   sprout with grass? Job 38:25–27 . . . . Job
Does the rain have a father? Job 38:28 . . . . Job
Who fathers the drops of dew? Job 38:28 . . . . Job
From whose womb comes the ice? Job 38:29 . . . . Job
Who gives birth to the frost from the heavens,
   when the waters become hard as stone, when the
   surface of the deep is frozen? Job 38:29–30 . . . . Job
Can you bind the chains of the Pleiades? Job 38:31 . . . . . . Job
Can you loosen Orion's belt? Job 38:31 . . . . Job
Can you bring forth the constellations in
   their seasons or lead out the Bear with its
   cubs? Job 38:32 . . . . Job
Do you know the laws of the heavens? Job 38:33 . . . . Job
Can you set up God's dominion over the earth?
   Job 38:33 . . . . Job
Can you raise your voice to the clouds and cover
   yourself with a flood of water? Job 38:34 . . . . Job
Do you send the lightning bolts on their way? Job 38:35 . . Job
Do they report to you, "Here we are"? Job 38:35 . . . . Job
Who gives the ibis wisdom or gives
   the rooster understanding? Job 38:36 . . . . Job
Who has the wisdom to count the clouds? Job 38:37 . . . . . Job

Can anyone capture it by the eyes, or trap it
   and pierce its nose? Job 40:24 . . . . Job
Can you pull in Leviathan with a fishhook
   or tie down its tongue with a rope? Job 41:1 . . . . Job
Can you put a cord through its nose or
   pierce its jaw with a hook? Job 41:2. . . . . Job
Will it keep begging you for mercy? Job 41:3. . . . . Job
Will it speak to you with gentle words? Job 41:3 . . . . Job
Will it make an agreement with you for you
   to take it as your slave for life? Job 41:4. . . . . Job
Can you make a pet of it like a bird or
   put it on a leash for the young women
   in your house? Job 41:5 . . . . Job
Will traders barter for it? Job 41:6 . . . . Job
Will they divide it up among the merchants? Job 41:6. . . . Job
Can you fill its hide with harpoons or its
   head with fishing spears? Job 41:7. . . . . Job
Who then is able to stand against me? Job 41:10. . . . . Job
Who has a claim against me that I must pay? Job 41:11 . . Job
Who can strip off its outer coat? Job 41:13 . . . . Job
Who would penetrate its double
   coat of armor? Job 41:13 . . . . Job
Who dares open the doors of his mouth,
   ringed about with his fearsome teeth? Job 41:14. . . . . . . Job
Who is this that obscures my plans without
   knowledge? Job 42:3 . . . . Job
What right have you to recite my laws or take
   my covenant on your lips? Psalm 50:16 . . . . The wicked
The multitude of your sacrifices—
   what are they to me? Isaiah 1:11 . . . . Israelites
When you come to appear before me,
   who has asked this of you—this trampling
   of my courts? Isaiah 1:12 . . . . Israelites

What do you mean by crushing my people
   and grinding the faces of the poor? Isaiah 3:15 . . . . Israelites
What more could have been done for my vineyard

than I have done for it? Isaiah 5:4 . . . Dwellers of Jerusalem
When I looked for good grapes,
   why did it yield only bad? Isaiah 5:4...Dwellers of Jerusalem
Whom shall I send? Isaiah 6:8 . . . . Isaiah
And who will go for us? Isaiah 6:8 . . . . Isaiah
What troubles you now, that you have all
   gone up on the roofs, you town so full of
   commotion, you city of tumult and
   revelry? Isaiah 22:1–2 . . . . People of Jerusalem
Who is it you have insulted and blasphemed?
   Isaiah 37:23 NIV 1984 . . . . Sennacherib
Against whom have you raised your voice
   and lifted your eyes in pride? Isaiah 37:23 . . . . . Sennacherib
Have you not heard? Isaiah 37:26 . . . . Sennacherib
To whom will you compare me? Isaiah 40:25 . . . . Israel
Or who is my equal? Isaiah 40:25 . . . . Israel
Who created all these? Isaiah 40:26 . . . . Israel
Why do you complain, Jacob? Why do you say,
   Israel, "My way is hidden from the Lord;
   my cause is disregarded by my God"? Isaiah 40:27 . . . Israel
Do you not know? Isaiah 40:28 . . . . Israel
Have you not heard? Isaiah 40:28 . . . . Israel
Who has stirred up one from the east, calling him
   in righteousness to his service? Isaiah 41:2 . . . . Israel
Who has done this and carried it through, calling
   forth the generations from the beginning? Isaiah 41:4 . Israel
Who told of this from the beginning, so we
   could know, or beforehand, so we could
   say, "He was right"? Isaiah 41:26 . . . . Israel
Who is blind but my servant, and deaf like the
   messenger I send? Isaiah 42:19 . . . . Israel
Who is blind like the one in covenant with me,
   blind like the servant of the Lord? Isaiah 42:19 . . . . . Israel
When I act, who can reverse it? Isaiah 43:13 . . . . Israel
Now it springs up; do you not perceive it? Isaiah 43:19 . Israel
Who then is like me? Isaiah 44:7 . . . . Israel
Did I not proclaim this and foretell it long ago?
   Isaiah 44:8 . . . . Israel

For where is the wrath of the oppressor? Isaiah 51:13 . . Israel
And now what do I have here? Isaiah 52:5 . . . . Himself
Why spend money on what is not bread, and your
    labor on what does not satisfy? Isaiah 55:2 . . . . Israel
Who are you mocking? Isaiah 57:4 . . . . Israel
At whom do you sneer and stick out your tongue?
    Isaiah 57:4 . . . . Israel
Are you not a brood of rebels, the offspring of liars?
    Isaiah 57:4 . . . . Israel
In view of all this, should I relent? Isaiah 57:6 . . . . Israel
Whom have you so dreaded and feared that you
    have not been true to me, and have neither
    remembered me nor taken this to heart? Isaiah 57:11 . . . Israel
Is it not because I have long been silent that
    you do not fear me? Isaiah 57:11 . . . . Israel
Is this the kind of fast I have chosen, only a
    day for people to humble themselves? Isaiah 58:5 . . . . Israel
Is it only for bowing one's head like a reed and
    for lying in sackcloth and ashes? Isaiah 58:5 . . . . Israel
Is that what you call a fast, a day acceptable
    to the LORD? Isaiah 58:5 . . . . Israel
Is not this the kind of fasting I have chosen:
    to loose the chains of injustice and untie the
    cords of the yoke, to set the oppressed free and
    break every yoke? Isaiah 58:6. . . . . Israel
Is it not to share your food with the hungry and to
    provide the poor wanderer with shelter—when you
    see the naked, to clothe them, and not to turn away
    from your own flesh and blood? Isaiah 58:7 . . . . Israel
Who are these that fly along like clouds,
    like doves to their nests? Isaiah 60:8 . . . . Israel
Where is the house you will build for me? Isaiah 66:1 . . . Israel
Where will my resting place be? Isaiah 66:1. . . . . Israel
Has not my hand made all these things,
    and so they came into being? Isaiah 66:2. . . . . Israel
Who has ever heard of such things? Isaiah 66:8. . . . . . . Israel
Who has ever seen things like this? Isaiah 66:8 . . . . Israel

Then why do I see every strong man with his
hands on his stomach like a woman in . . . .
labor, every face turned deathly pale? Jeremiah 30:6. . . Israel
Why do you cry out over your wound, your pain
that has no cure? Jeremiah 30:15. . . . . Israel
I will bring him near and he will come close
to me—for who is he who will devote
himself to be close to me? Jeremiah 30:21. . . . . Israel
Is not Ephraim my dear son, the child in
whom I delight? Jeremiah 31:20 . . . . Israel
How long will you wander, unfaithful Daughter
Israel? Jeremiah 31:22 . . . . Israel
Is anything too hard for me? Jeremiah 32:27 . . . . . . .Jeremiah
Have you not noticed that these people are saying,
"The LORD has rejected the two kingdoms
he chose"? Jeremiah 33:24. .Jeremiah
Will you not learn a lesson and obey my words?
Jeremiah 35:13. . . . . Israel
Why bring such great disaster on yourselves by
cutting off from Judah the men and women,
the children and infants, and so leave yourselves
without a remnant? Jeremiah 44:7. . . . . Israel
Why arouse my anger with what your hands have
made, burning incense to other gods in Egypt,
where you have come to live? Jeremiah 44:8 . . . . Israel
Have you forgotten the wickedness committed by your
ancestors and by the kings and queens of Judah and the
wickedness committed by you and your wives in the land
of Judah and the streets of Jerusalem? Jeremiah 44:9. . .Israel
What do I see? Jeremiah 46:5. . . . . Himself
Who is this that rises like the Nile, like
rivers of surging waters? Jeremiah 46:7 . . . . .Pharaoh's army
Why will your warriors be laid low?
Jeremiah 46:15. Egypt and Migdol
How can you say, "We are warriors,
men valiant in battle"? Jeremiah 48:14 . . . . Moabites
What has happened? Jeremiah 48:19 . . . . .Escapees
Was not Israel the object of your ridicule?
Jeremiah 48:27. . . . . Moabites

Is it a trivial matter for the people of Judah
    to do the detestable things they are doing
    here? Ezekiel 8:17 . . . . Ezekiel
Must they also fill the land with violence and
    continually arouse my anger? Ezekiel 8:17 . . . . Ezekiel
Son of man, did not the Israelites, that rebellious
    people, ask you, "What are you doing?" Ezekiel 12:9 . . . Ezekiel
Son of man, what is this proverb you have in
    the land of Israel: "The days go by and every
    vision comes to nothing"? Ezekiel 12:22 . . . . Ezekiel
Have you not seen false visions and uttered lying
    divinations when you say, "The LORD declares,"
    though I have not spoken? Ezekiel 13:7 . . . . . . False prophets
Will you ensnare the lives of my people but
    preserve your own? Ezekiel 13:18 . . . . False prophets
Should I let them inquire of me at all? Ezekiel 14:3 . . . Ezekiel
Son of man, how is the wood of a vine different
    from that of a branch from any of the trees
    in the forest? Ezekiel 15:2 . . . . Ezekiel
Is wood ever taken from it to make anything useful?
    Ezekiel 15:3 . . . . Ezekiel
Do they make pegs from it to hang things on?
    Ezekiel 15:3 . . . . Ezekiel
And after it is thrown on the fire as fuel and the
    fire burns both ends and chars the middle,
    is it then useful for anything? Ezekiel 15:4 . . . . Ezekiel
If it was not useful for anything when it was whole,
    how much less can it be made into something useful
    when the fire has burned it and it is charred?
    Ezekiel 15:5 . . . . Ezekiel
Was your prostitution not enough?
    Ezekiel 16:20 . . . . People of Jerusalem
Did you not add lewdness to all your other
    detestable practices? Ezekiel 16:43 . . . . People of Jerusalem
Will it thrive? Ezekiel 17:9 . . . . Israelites
Will it not be uprooted and stripped of its fruit
    so that it withers? Ezekiel 17:9 . . . . Israelites
It has been planted, but will it thrive? Ezekiel 17:10. Israelites

Will not the land tremble for this, and all
who live in it mourn? Amos 8:8 . . . . Amos
Are not you Israelites the same to me as
the Cushites? Amos 9:7. . . . . .Israelites
Did I not bring Israel up from Egypt,
the Philistines from Caphtor and the
Arameans from Kir? Amos 9:7 . . . . Israel
If thieves came to you, if robbers in the night—
oh, what a disaster awaits you!—would they
not steal only as much as they wanted? Obadiah 1:5. . .Edom
If grape pickers came to you, would they not
leave a few grapes? Obadiah 1:5 . . . . Edom
"In that day," declares the LORD, "will I not
destroy the wise men of Edom?" Obadiah 1:8. . . . . . .Edom
Is it right for you to be angry? Jonah 4:4 . . . . Jonah
Is it right for you to be angry about the plant? Jonah 4:9. . .Jonah
Should I not have concern for the great city
of Nineveh? Jonah 4:11 . . . . Jonah
Do not my words do good to the one whose
ways are upright? Micah 2:7 . . . . Judah
Why do you now cry aloud. . . ? Micah 4:9. . . . . Israel
Have you no king? Micah 4:9. Israel
Has your ruler perished, that pain seizes you like
that of a woman in labor? Micah 4:9 . . . . Israel
My people, what have I done to you? Micah 6:3 . . . . . . Israel
How have I burdened you? Micah 6:3 . . . . Israel
Am I still to forget your ill-gotten treasures,
you wicked house, and the short ephah,
which is accursed? Micah 6:10 . . . . Israel
Shall I acquit someone with dishonest scales,
with a bag of false weights? Micah 6:11 . . . . Israel
Will not all of them taunt him with ridicule and scorn,
saying, "Woe to him who piles up stolen goods and
makes himself wealthy by extortion!"? Habakkuk 2:6. .Israel
How long must this go on? Habakkuk 2:6. . . . . Israel
Will not your creditors suddenly arise? Habakkuk 2:7. . Israel
Will they not wake up and make you tremble?
Habakkuk 2:7 . . . . Israel

When you bring blind animals for sacrifice,
    is that not wrong? Malachi 1:8 niv 1984. . . . . . . The people
When you sacrifice crippled or diseased animals,
    is that not wrong? Malachi 1:8 niv 1984. . . . . . . The people
Would he be pleased with you? Malachi 1:8. . . . . . The people
Would he accept you? Malachi 1:8 . . . . The people
With such offerings from your hands,
    will he accept you? Malachi 1:9 . . . . The people
When you bring injured, crippled or diseased
    animals and offer them as sacrifices, should I
    accept them from your hands?
    Malachi 1:13 niv 1984 . . . . The people
Will a man rob God? Malachi 3:8 niv 1984 . . . . . The people
Then who will get what you have prepared
    for yourself? Luke 12:20 . . . . The rich man
Where, O death, is your victory?
    1 Corinthians 15:55 (quoted by Paul) . . . . Death
Where, O death, is your sting?
    1 Corinthians 15:55 (quoted by Paul) . . . . Death

INSPIRATION FOR EVERY DAY!

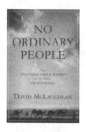

No Ordinary People
This book features 100 in-depth, easy-to-read entries on the people behind the scenes, the everyday men and women, not the kings, queens, miracle workers, or leaders. These people, from the Good Samaritan to Pilate's wife, played a powerful role in God's plan for humanity and their stories were recorded for our benefit today.
Paperback / 978-1-63409-119-0 / $9.99

Everyday Moments with God
This lovely prayer collection is designed for those "everyday moments" in a woman's life—the tired moments, the stressed-out moments, the joyful moments, the tearful moments, the peaceful and chaotic moments. . . Dozens of practical and encouraging prayers, complemented by related scripture selections, will inspire women of all ages to strengthen their heart-connection to the heavenly Father.
Paperback / 978-1-63409-132-9 / $4.99

Expanded Editions of
The Bible Promise Book®
Just for Women

The Bible Promise Book® for Women—
Prayer and Praise Edition
This great title is now available in a deluxe, expanded Prayer and Praise Edition for women featuring the beloved King James Version of the Bible plus encouraging prayers and inspiring hymn lyrics. With dozens of relevant topics—including Comfort, Faith, Hope, Joy, Love—women will find hundreds of verses at their fingertips.
DiCarta / 978-1-62836-645-7 / $14.99

The Bible Promise Book® for Women—
Prayer Edition Journal
This delightful journal fits perfectly into a woman's prayer life. Featuring scripture, encouraging prayers, inspiring quotes, and generous journaling space, women of all ages won't be able to resist this lovely package. Journalers will find themselves encouraged and inspired to record all of the ways they are blessed and loved by their heavenly Father.
DiCarta / 978-1-63409-075-9 / $16.99